# Food MeN Love

### Margie Lapanja

## Foreword by Mario Batali

Gramercy Books
New York

To *Ambrosia Lené Healy,*

who loves men

This 2001 edition is published by Gramercy™ Books, a division of Random House Value Publishing, Inc., 280 Park Avenue, New York, NY 10017, by arrangement with Conari Press.

Gramercy™ Books and design are registered trademarks of Random House Value Publishing, Inc.

Random House
New York • Toronto • London • Sydney • Auckland
http://www.randomhouse.com/

Printed and bound in the United States of America

**Library of Congress Cataloging-in-Publication Data**

Lapanja, Margie, 1959-
    Food men love / Margie Lapanja ; foreword by Mario Batali.
        p. cm.
    Originally published: Berkeley, Calif. : Conari Press, c2001.
    Includes bibliographical references and index.
    ISBN 0-517-21904-2 (alk. paper)
        1. Cookery. I. Title.

TX714 .L353 2001b
641.5—dc21

                                    2001042851

10 9 8 7 6 5 4 3 2 1

# Food Men Love

Foreword                                              v
Introduction: The **H**ighway to His **H**eart        1

Bread and **B**reakfast                               5
**W**arming Up His **A**ppetite                      35
Pasta, **P**izza, and Molto Risotto                  63
**F**owl Play                                        93
His Dish Is **F**ish                                113
Magnificent Meat and **P**otatoes                   137
Playing with **F**ire                               159
How **S**weet It Is                                 181

Red Letter Resources                                211
Acknowledgments                                     216
Works Cited                                         218
Index                                               221
Permissions                                         232

# Foreword

## by Mario Batali

Without resorting to cliché or insulting simplicity, Margie Lapanja has culled a remarkable wealth of recipes, food facts, trivia, and other proof that real men are about much more than burgers and beer. *Food Men Love* reads like an owner's manual for those three things: food, men, and, most important, love. Watch out, marriage counselors and divorce attorneys: This book may put you out of business.

---

**Mario Batali** is the host of *Molto Mario* on the TV Food Network, author of *Simple Italian Food: Recipes from My Two Villages* (Clarkson Potter, 1998) and *Mario Batali Holiday Food* (Clarkson Potter, 2000). He is the chef/owner of Babbo, Lupa, and Esca restaurants and Italian Wine Merchants in New York City.

**T**here is no sincerer love
than the love of food.

—George Bernard Shaw

# The Highway to His Heart

*The purpose of a cookery book is unmistak-
able. Its object can conceivably be no other
than to increase the happiness of mankind.*

—Joseph Conrad

B efore sex, before sports, before Corvettes, Hummers, and
Harleys—before the beginning of recorded time—men have loved
food. They have loved how its taste soothed them, they have loved who
made it for them, and they have enjoyed how important they felt
when it was served to them. As children, food made them feel nourished and happy. As adults, men thrived on the thrill of the hunt, the
satisfaction of providing a bountiful meal, and the fortitude of cama-
raderie at the feast. Food and love, hunger and passion, pleasure and
fulfillment have always preoccupied the male psyche and soul.

The great statesman, Winston Churchill, was known to ascribe satisfaction and happiness in his life to "hot baths, cold champagne, new

peas, old brandy." Across the ocean, as Churchill basked, President Harry Truman's love of tuna noodle casserole endeared him to a nation of homemakers: If it was good for Harry, it was good for their husbands. The great mythological gods of yore drew their sustenance and power from debauching on nectar and ambrosia, while action hero Popeye claimed spinach made him "good to the finich" and polished it off straight from the can. And, of course, the fate of mankind was sealed when ol' Adam of Eden simply could not resist taking a big bite of Eve's sweet, juicy apple when she offered it to him—or was that a slice of apple pie?

*Food Men Love* is a lively tribute to men and the tastes that make them happy—an entire cookbook dedicated to men's favorite foods. Since the day when, as a young girl, I discovered that I could trade cookies for privileged information and access (like the location of and honorary entry into the "No girls allowed" secret fort) from the boys in the neighborhood, I have been intrigued with the effects of food on the male body and spirit. For years, I owned and operated bakeries, spending my days gathering stories, recipes, and insights while experimenting with and preparing favorite foods and observing their results. I consequently now find myself particularly interested in the aphrodisiacal qualities of certain unconventional "love potions"—cinnamon rolls, apple pie, tiramisu, and any most cherished or desired fare—and truly enjoy talking to men about the foods they love and serving it forth.

To truly understand a man, I believe it is essential to know the foods that jumpstart his heart—the foods that satisfy his soul, pleasure his senses, and make him feel nourished, strong, and comforted. Grandma knew it too: The sure-fire way to keep a man's *heart on* is to fire him up through his stomach.

When interviewing hundreds of men for this book—via e-mail, letters, in person, over the phone—I asked two simple questions:

**1** What foods do you *love* to eat (What you would want if you were to request your "last meal"?), and

**2** Do you have a favorite dish or recipe you like to prepare?

Besides a few cheeky requests for *Nascargo, Testosteroni,* or *MANicotti,* most men wanted an honest serving of a favored food that turned them on: yes, meat and potatoes, divine desserts, comfort foods, food that Mom made, breakfasts in bed, grilled fare. In fact, at one point in my cookbook research process, I had over 200 recipes and requests for meat dishes—and two for vegetables. The rest is culinary fodder and history.

Though I can't lay any grand scientific or sociological food claim to fame, I will tell you this: In general, men love their meat, they prefer to *be* served rather than *to* serve, and the food they love to eat is immeasurably different than the food they like to cook. And though the overall zest of the book might tend to reflect the tastes of the hundreds of gentlemen I interviewed and entertained, I did keep the other 3,058,028,688 males in the world in mind—and do hope to hear from them someday, too!

The recipes in these pages are tried-and-true man-pleasers, the "best of the best." Among the signature recipes of esteemed chefs and kitchen wizards, there are favorite feel-good feasts of superstars, sports heroes, luminaries, grill gurus, starving artists, burger kings, and every man in between. Throughout, I've sprinkled in some interesting food lore and tantalizing tidbits for the reader to enjoy and savor, and I also tossed in a few practical aphrodisiacs from several kitchen goddesses for good measure. As for the recipe content, I make no apologies. I am merely the messenger reporting from the ranks and a few Mobil five-star kitchens on the side. At its finest, though perhaps not gourmet to the gills, this book affords a captivating glance at the gastronomic universe of man.

*Food Men Love* is about the epicurean glories of indulging in favorite, beloved dishes and basking in the satisfaction that eating them brings. It is a delicious romp for the senses stirred up for all the men out there who were hoping for sexual favors and a leather jacket for their birthdays but ended up with a "King of the Grill" apron, matching mitts, and this cookbook instead. In essence, this spirited anthology of the honest pleasures of men's lives and palates is an open invitation to all men and those who love and cook for them to be more creative, passionate, and playful in the kitchen and in every aspect of life. *Food Men Love* is the *highway* to a man's heart for those who choose to cruise. Do enjoy the ride!

# Bread
## and
# Breakfast

All happiness depends
on a leisurely breakfast.
—John Gunther

*Feel-Good Fare to Jump-Start His Heart*

HE LOVES . . .

**B**acon and eggs. There are few sights that appeal to me more than the streaks of lean and fat in good side bacon. . . . Nothing is quite as intoxicating as the smell of bacon frying in the morning, save perhaps for the smell of coffee brewing.—*James Beard,* Beard on Food

**P**ancakes and sausage. That's it.—*Charles, Arizona*

**F**igs and buttery mascarpone cheese with some honey and pistachio nuts. This is something you will want to try.—*Terry, Italy*

**A** soft-boiled egg and a croissant, half a grapefruit, and a café au lait in a cup the size of a cereal bowl.—*Michael, New York and Florida*

**C**rab cakes Benedict, Dutch pancakes, sourdough bread, and bananas with honey and cream.—*Karl, California*

## The Real Way to Rise *and* Shine

Even with the onslaught of protein shakes and high-powered breakfast bars, Wheaties™ has defended its title, the "Breakfast of Champions," brilliantly for nearly a century. If we believe what the all-stars on the Wheaties boxes tell us, we are on our way to a win-win, grand-slam day every time we fill our bowls with these golden flakes. Life is the prize, so eat your Wheaties and *carpe diem!*

But if it is the *moment* rather than the entire day you wish to seize—let's say you're in a robust mood and want to start your day with a little hanky-panky—leave your cereal bowl empty and your jock strap off. The time is right to fire up with the newly scientifically proven "breakfast of lovers"—the cinnamon roll!

That's right. In one study by sex researchers, the penile blood flow of thirty-one healthy male subjects was measured when they whiffed a range of fragrances from perfume to roses to suntan oil to black licorice. Every odor boosted the flow from one level to another, but some fragrances hit the jackpot, so to speak. Among the supererotic turn-ons were the aromas of pumpkin pie, lavender, and doughnuts. Let it be known, however, that the supreme seductress of all smells proved to be that of the sexy, spice-laced cinnamon roll. And you thought you needed a protein shake. . . .

# $\mathcal{S}$*ensuous* **C***innamon* **R***olls*

**The Dough**

3 cups unbleached flour

1½ tablespoons baking powder

½ teaspoon salt

¼ teaspoon ground cardamom

½ cup (1 stick) cold, unsalted butter

1 cup warm milk

**Glaze**

2 cups powdered sugar

1 tablespoon orange

2 tablespoons milk

**Filling**

1 cup raisins

1 to 2 teaspoons orange zest

2 tablespoons rum

1 cup raw sugar

1 cup brown sugar

2 tablespoons milk

3 tablespoons ground cinnamon

1 teaspoon ground nutmeg

½ cup melted butter

1 cup shelled pecans, coarsely
  chopped

---

To make the dough, combine flour, baking powder, salt, and cardamom in a large bowl; blend well. Cut the cold butter into the flour mixture with a pastry blender or fork until mixture becomes granular. Add the milk and stir with a fork until a soft dough forms.

Turn the dough out on a lightly floured surface, knead 10 to 12 times, and pat into a rectangle. Wrap and refrigerate while you prepare the filling.

To prepare the filling, soak the raisins and orange zest in rum. In a separate bowl, combine the two kinds of sugars, milk, and spices. Prepare two 8-inch round pans (or one 9 x 13-inch rectangular pan) by brushing the bottom with some of the melted butter, and sprinkle enough sugar mixture on the bottom of each pan to cover the surface evenly (about ¼ cup for each). Reserve the rest of the sugar mixture.

Preheat the oven to 400°F. On a lightly floured surface, roll the dough into a large ¼-inch thick, 12 x 18-inch rectangle, with the "long" side near you.

Brush the dough with the remaining melted butter and sprinkle the remaining sugar mixture evenly over the dough, followed by the raisin mixture and pecans. Starting with the longer edge, loosely roll the dough toward you, "jelly roll" style. Using a very sharp knife cut the dough into 1 to 1¼-inch slices and place them in the pan spiral side up and slightly apart.

Bake for 20 to 25 minutes, until the rolls are golden brown. While the rolls are baking, make the glaze by combining all ingredients in a small bowl. When the cinnamon rolls are hot out of the oven, invert the pan immediately onto a serving tray. Drizzle glaze over them and indulge! Makes 14 to 16 sinfully delicious cinnamon rolls.

*Knowing you is such delicious torment.*

—Ralph Waldo Emerson

# Life Is Fine *with the* Cinnamon Girl

Scientists may have discovered what the sweet smell of cinnamon *does* to increase a man's virility and blood flow, but have they given us a good reason *why?* As a kitchen courtesan, I say the answer is simple: Cinnamon is an *aphrodisiac.*

Myth holds that Aphrodite, the Greek goddess of love, could harness the alchemical powers of her insignia spice at will, delivering its wallop on unsuspecting mortal men whenever she needed a little adoration. "Cinnamon Girl" simply sprinkled it on their food. After she won the coveted Golden Apple at the Judgment of Paris—the infamous beauty pageant of the great goddesses that incited the Trojan War—that noble fruit (now the naughty orb of temptation) also fell under her command. With apples in one basket and mounds of cinnamon in the other, no man was above the call of Aphrodite.

Are you a believer? If the Sensuous Cinnamon Rolls didn't increase your pulse this morning, the French Stud Muffins will. They are laced with the two vital aphrodisiacal ingredients, they are delightful to eat in bed . . . and they're French. *Mais oui!*

*An aphrodisiac is anything you think it is.*

—Dr. Ruth Westheimer

# French Stud Muffins

**Muffins**
4½ cups unbleached flour
1¾ cups sugar
1 tablespoon baking powder
¾ teaspoon salt
¾ teaspoon ground nutmeg
1½ cups milk
3 eggs

1 cup margarine, melted
1 cup apples, peeled, and finely
    chopped or grated

**Topping**
1 cup sugar
1 tablespoon cinnamon
3 tablespoons melted butter

---

Preheat oven to 350°F. Mix all dry ingredients listed under "Muffins" together by hand, forming a "well" in the center of a large bowl. Whisk together the milk and eggs in a separate bowl and then pour them into the dry mixture. Mix gently, dribbling the melted margarine into the equation as you go, until all ingredients come together. (To avoid tough, cone-headed muffins, do not overmix.) Gently fold in the apples.

Scoop dough into a muffin tin lined with paper cups, filling the cups to the top. Bake for 20 to 25 minutes or until a toothpick comes out clean.

While muffins are baking, prepare the topping by mixing together the sugar and cinnamon. Immediately after taking the muffins out of the oven, brush the tops with melted butter and shake a storm of cinnamon-sugar on top. Makes a bountiful 13 (baker's dozen) aphrodisiacs disguised as muffins; prepare for the effects.

# A Marriage Made with **B***anana* **B***read?*

In his book *The White House Family Cookbook,* White House executive chef and author Henry Haller entertains with recipes and tales of presidential palatal preferences and favorite foods of first families, all woven together with Americana food lore and good inside dish, like what favorite fare Ronnie Reagan had delivered to the hospital when he was recovering from his gunshot wound (I'll tell you later in the book . . . ).

The sweetest story is that of David and Julie Nixon Eisenhower. Later to marry, they first met as eight-year-olds. David, Ike's young son, was a hearty eater who loved banana bread. Since Mrs. Nixon adored bananas, her first daughter, Julie, also grew up with banana bread as a Number One favorite. Same White House, same chef, same recipe. It was "very, very, very, very good," David once wrote in a thank-you note to the chef. I bet this very, very good banana bread will put stars in any man's eyes.

*Kissin' don't last; cookery do!*

—George Meredith

# Bet On It Banana Bread

### A favorite of the Eisenhowers

4 cups unbleached flour

2 cups brown sugar

1 teaspoon salt

1 teaspoon baking soda

4 eggs

2 teaspoons pure vanilla extract

⅔ cup buttermilk

1 cup margarine, melted

4 large, very ripe bananas, mashed

2 cups of your favorite nuts, chopped
(optional)

Additional brown sugar and chopped
nuts (optional)

---

Preheat oven to 350°F. Grease and flour two 8 x 4-inch loaf pans. (If you prefer muffins, line tin with muffin cups.) Combine flour, brown sugar, salt, and baking soda in a large bowl. Make a well in the center.

In a separate bowl, whisk together the eggs, vanilla, and buttermilk. Pour into the dry mixture and blend slightly, always by hand with a wooden spoon. Add the melted margarine and mix a bit more. Finally, add mashed bananas and, if using, nuts. Mix gently until ingredients are blended (do not overmix). Spoon batter into the prepared pans and sprinkle the top with additional brown sugar and nuts, if desired.

Bake for 45 to 55 minutes (20 to 25 minutes for muffins). To check if the muffins are done, insert a toothpick; if it comes out clean, the bread is done. Note the baking time for the future. Turn out to cool. Slice and serve with butter. Makes 2 loaves or 14 muffins.

## Stirring It Up *with the* **Big Boys**

What does a celebrated New York chef and author do when he's not overseeing his culinary creations at one of the grandest establishments in New York City? Does he hobnob with fellow wizards talking *foie gras* and *quattro formaggi* while sipping fine wine and swapping tales of gastronomic escapades in Paris, Saint-Père-sous-Vezelay, and Brussels?

Daniel Orr, Executive Chef at New York's Guastavino's, author of *Real Food,* and former cuisine king at La Grenouille, bakes his grandmother's biscuits. 'Tis true; for occasional weekend brunches and holiday breakfasts, he rolls up his sleeves, puts on his apron, and pays tribute to Gramma Orr.

Ever since I discovered that Chef Orr developed his childhood taste buds in the culinary training ground of Indiana (as did I), I've been a fan. I love that someone from the land of meatloaf and coleslaw has been transformed into such a fine, respected chef. He was surely inspired back in the Hoosier state by some of the best buttermilk biscuits you'll ever taste, thanks to his grandma.

> *Simple pleasures are essential pleasures,*
> *restorative, necessary to survival.*
>
> —Jacqueline Deval, Reckless Appetites

# *G*ramma **O**rr's **B**uttermilk **B**iscuits

| | |
|---|---|
| 2 cups unbleached white flour | 1 generous teaspoon sugar |
| 1 tablespoon baking powder | ½ cup (1 stick) cold unsalted butter |
| ¼ teaspoon soda | ¾ to 1 cup cold buttermilk |
| ½ teaspoon salt | |

Preheat the oven to 450°F. In a medium bowl, thoroughly combine the dry ingredients. Cut in the cold butter with a sharp pastry cutter, leaving some large pea-sized pieces among the other cornmeal-sized pieces.

Add the buttermilk and toss to combine (do not overmix or they will become tough and dry!); form a ball. Knead the dough lightly, pat it out to a ¾-inch thickness, and cut with a biscuit cutter. Bake biscuits on an ungreased baking sheet at 450°F for 2 to 3 minutes, reduce heart to 350°F, and bake for another 8 to 9 minutes. Makes a dozen or so grandma-style biscuits.

## THE INSIDE LINE

At Guastavino's, Chef Orr transforms his grandma's biscuits into a fabuous dessert. He simply brushes them with buttermilk and sprinkles raw sugar and sweet spices on them before baking. They are served sliced and topped with local Tri-Star strawberries, crème fraîche, and a little chopped mint.

# Flipped Out *for a* Johnny Cake

The first colonists in America were simply smitten with the newly discovered Indian crop called "corn." England had its porridges, puddings, and muffins, but Old World tables had never known the likes of such rustic, soulful creations as stone-ground cornmeal being flipped, fried, and cooked in the New World.

To founding father Benjamin Franklin, cornmeal in any of its incarnations was soul food. In fact, during a visit to London in 1768 to plead the case for the colonies, he begged his daughter to send him the foods for which he was homesick, among them cornmeal. Ben would give cooking classes to the Englishwomen, enthusiastically teaching them how to make cornbread or flip an Indian slapjack. When he and the colonists were publicly jeered by a *London Gazette* journalist for eating food that could never afford "an agreeable breakfast," ol' Ben planted the seeds of separatism by boldly rebutting, "Permit me, an American, to inform the British gentleman, who seems ignorant of the matter . . . that our johnny cake or hoe cake, hot from the fire, is better than a Yorkshire muffin." Any day.

Spread some warm, melting butter and Barbara's Jalapeño Jelly on his beloved corn bread, and loyal Ben would have been talking *revolution*.

> *The destiny of a nation depends upon how and what they eat.*
>
> —Brillat-Savarin

15

# Johnny Cake Corn Bread

### Benjamin Franklin's favorite

| | |
|---|---|
| 1½ cups stone-ground cornmeal | 2 eggs |
| 1 cup unbleached flour | 1 cup sour cream |
| ¼ cup brown sugar | ½ cup milk |
| 1 teaspoon salt | ¼ cup margarine or butter, melted |
| ½ teaspoon baking soda | ⅔ cup creamed corn (or freshly cooked |
| 1 tablespoon baking powder | corn from the kernel) |

Preheat oven to 400°F. In a large bowl and by hand, combine the dry ingredients. In a separate bowl, whisk together the eggs, sour cream, and milk. Pour this mixture into the dry mix and stir gently. Pour in the melted margarine and mix slightly. Fold in the creamed corn.

Pour the batter into a 10-inch, greased cast iron skillet. Bake for approximately 20 minutes or until a toothpick comes out clean. (You can also cook this batter "pancake style" in a stove top skillet to make authentic corn johnny cakes; cook each side of the johnny cake for a minute or two.) Makes 6 to 8 servings.

# ℬarbara's Jalapeño Jelly

| | |
|---|---|
| One 3½-ounce can jalapeño peppers | 6 cups white sugar |
| 1 large bell pepper, seeded and sliced | One 6-ounce package Certo™ pectin |
| One 4-ounce can chiles | (use both pouches) |
| 1 cup white vinegar | |

In a blender, blend together on high speed the two kinds of peppers, chiles, and vinegar. In a large saucepan over medium heat, combine the pepper blend with the sugar and stir until the sugar completely dissolves. Add the Certo pectin and bring to a rolling boil. Boil for 3 minutes, stirring constantly.

To preserve, pour the jelly into hot, sterilized jars and top with canning lids sealed with bands (see the Inside Line below). Store in a cool area and refrigerate after opening. Makes 6 half-pint jars of Barbara's zesty jelly.

## THE INSIDE LINE

You skipped home ec class in high school? Here's a quick canning lesson from *James Villas' The Town and Country Cookbook:*

Unscrew ring bands from canning jars, remove lids; arrange jars in a large pot, and cover with water. Bring water to a boil, cover, and sterilize jars for 10 minutes. Remove jars from the water with clean tongs and pack [with Barbara's Jalapeño Jelly], taking care not to touch the insides of the [sterilized] jars. Wipe rims clean with paper towels.

[Using the tongs] dip the sealing lids into the hot water used for sterilizing jars, [place lids on top of the filled jars] and screw ring bands on tightly.

Place the jars in a draft-free area until the lids "ping" and remain down when pushed with a finger [signs they are sterile].

Do not fret if the lid doesn't do its "ping thing" and remains convex; just store in the refrigerator and enjoy!

## AND ALL THE PRESIDENTS' PANCAKES

Pancakes, a true American tradition, have made their mark throughout history. Thomas Jefferson was so smitten with his griddlecakes that accompanied his fried apples and bacon and eggs that he brought his governess to the White House from Monticello mainly because she had a magic touch at flipping the cakes.

President Andrew Jackson was partial to buckwheat-cornmeal flapjacks; Franklin D. Roosevelt swore by hot, buttered maple syrup on plain, fluffy pancakes; and Ike loved cornmeal johnny cakes smothered in light molasses. Even spendthrift Calvin Coolidge caught on to the power of the pancake and traditionally had low-cost buckwheat breakfast cakes served at morning meetings.

# Mining *for a* Silver-Dollar Breakfast

Before Sam Clemens became Mark Twain, he was a cub reporter in the mining town of Virginia City, Nevada, writing for the local newspaper under the *nom de plume* "Josh."

In his own words, Josh tells us what a real breakfast meant to him: "A mighty porterhouse steak an inch and a half thick, hot and sputtering from the grill; dusted with fragrant pepper; enriched with little melting bits of butter . . . archipelagoed with mushrooms . . . and a great cup of American homemade coffee . . . some smoking hot biscuits, and a plate of hot buckwheat [pan] cakes, with transparent syrup. . . ."

After the sun rose over the High Sierra, the young Mark Twain would head off to work and proceed to weave wonder-words with his trusty typewriter. His editor's only instructions were, "Write so damned well the miners will read the *Enterprise* before they drink their liquor, court their women, or dig their gold." Which he did . . . after he ate his bonanza in pancakes.

# *Silver Dollar Slapjacks with Wild Blue Sauce*

A favorite of Mark Twain

**Slapjacks**

1 cup buttermilk

¼ cup milk

1 large egg, room temperature

2 tablespoons butter, melted, or canola oil

1 cup unbleached white flour

1 tablespoon sugar

1 teaspoon baking powder

½ teaspoon baking soda

¼ teaspoon salt

Nonstick canola oil cooking spray

**Wild Blue Sauce**

1½ cups fresh wild blueberries (cultivated or frozen berries will do in a pinch)

⅓ cup brown sugar

2 to 3 tablespoons lemon juice, freshly squeezed (no substitutes)

½ teaspoon crystallized ginger, finely chopped

Dash of ground nutmeg

---

Get the sauce going first. To make the blueberry sauce, combine all listed ingredients in a saucepan and bring to a slow, bubbly boil over medium heat. Reduce heat to low and simmer for about 5 minutes, until the sauce begins to thicken and its sweet aroma fills the air.

To make the pancake batter, whisk together in a large bowl the buttermilk, milk, egg, and melted butter. In a separate, smaller bowl or measuring cup, blend together the flour, sugar, baking powder, baking soda, and salt. Gently tap the dry ingredients into the buttermilk mixture and stir it up.

While the Wild Blue Sauce is gurgling, lightly spray or grease a griddle or nonstick skillet and heat it over medium-high heat. Ladle small 3-inch pools of batter onto the hot griddle. Cook the silver dollars for about one minute until teeny bubbles come to the surface, gently flip them, and cook for another 30 seconds.

To make a great impression, serve 3 stacks of 3 silver dollar pancakes on an extra large plate and top them with an eruption of the hot Wild Blue Sauce. Makes 16 to 18 pancakes.

*Get your facts first, and then you can*
*distort them as much as you please.*

—Mark Twain

## Treat That Poor Knight Like a King

Before French toast elevated its social status and found its way onto up-scale breakfast tables, it kept shady company on the edge of antiquity's kitchen. In the dank, dark days of England's Middle Ages, when poor knights and foot soldiers were out defending their king's lands and castle, they subsisted on stale slices of bread dipped in wine and soured milk and fried over a fire. The dish was aptly nicknamed "Poor Knights of Windsor."

Over in France, this same fare was (and still is) the classic *pain perdu*, or "lost bread," made exclusively with leftover bread from the baker's day off—bread that would normally be "lost" to the birds and dogs. Add a few eggs, sweet spices, rich milk . . . *voilà!* Men came to love it.

Whenever I want a man to feel *regal*, I cook up this remarkable, revamped version of Portuguese Toast with peachy Love Sauce from my book *Goddess in the Kitchen* and allow him the fantasy of being king of the world.

### King Toast with Queen Peach Sauce

| | |
|---|---|
| 4 large firm peaches or 8 apricots, peeled, pitted, sliced | 1 teaspoon ground nutmeg, divided |
| ¾ to 1 cup pure maple syrup | 1 round loaf King's Hawaiian Bread™ |
| | 4 eggs |

| | |
|---|---|
| 1 cup half-and-half or milk | ½ teaspoon pure vanilla extract |
| ½ teaspoon ground cinnamon | Butter for frying |

Place the fruit in a medium-sized saucepan, add maple syrup, and sprinkle ½ teaspoon nutmeg over everything. Cover and bring to a boil over medium-low heat. Once the syrup begins to boil, turn off the heat, but leave the saucepan on the burner to keep the nectar warm.

In the meanwhile, slice the loaf of bread in half, then cut 1-inch thick slices of bread of varied sizes from those halves (a loaf of King's provides 12 hefty slices). In a shallow bowl, whisk together the eggs, half-and-half or milk, cinnamon, vanilla, and remaining nutmeg.

Melt a dollop of butter in a skillet or on a griddle over medium-high heat. Dip both sides of the bread quickly in the egg mixture and fry for 2 to 3 minutes until golden brown; flip and fry the other side.

While the toast is frying, transfer the Queen Peach Sauce into a decorative bowl or gravy boat with a ladle. Serve toast on warmed plates. Makes 4 servings.

### THE INSIDE LINE

Feel free to substitute thawed frozen fruit or unsweetened canned fruit (drained) in place of the fresh; you will need about 2 cups of sliced peaches or apricots. Also, if there is no King's Hawaiian Bread on your local store shelves, substitute sweet French or Portuguese bread.

# You Can't Waffle on Character

If I were entertaining anyone of stature—a great chef, celebrity, luminary, politician, friend, or the Wizard of Oz himself—I would invite him to breakfast and enchant him with a huge plate of waffles with warm maple syrup, fresh fruit, cinnamon, sour cream, and sweet butter.

I say you can tell a man's character by his reaction to this crisp, forthright hot cake. I've discovered a "waffle man" is generally unpretentious, wholesome, hearty, fun-loving, and honest.

Alton Brown, the celebrity chef on the Food Network's television show *Good Eats,* says one of his favorite things to cook is "waffles—anytime, day or night." A waffle man. When Thomas Jefferson visited Holland, he brought back a "woffle" iron so he could enjoy them at Monticello. A waffle man. President Gerald Ford, bless his heart—a waffle man.

So all of you waffle men out there, heat your irons, and cook up a *great* waffle.

*You can tell a lot about a fellow's character*
*by his way of eating jellybeans.*

—Ronald Reagan

# Norwegian Belgian Waffles

2 cups milk

2 cups rolled oats (old-fashioned or quick)

2 large eggs, separated, at room temperature

2 tablespoons brown sugar or honey

2 tablespoons applesauce

2 tablespoons soft butter

½ cup whole wheat flour

½ cup unbleached white flour

1 tablespoon baking powder

½ teaspoon salt

---

Grease and preheat a Belgian waffle iron (a regular waffle iron also works perfectly). Either scald the milk in a saucepan over low heat and mix in the oats, or combine the oats and milk in a large bowl and microwave on HIGH for 3 to 4 minutes. Whisk in the egg yolks, brown sugar or honey, applesauce, and butter.

Beat the egg whites until a soft peak forms; set aside. In a small bowl (or right in the measuring cup to save time), blend together the two kinds of flours, baking powder, and salt. Tap the dry ingredients into the wet ingredients, stir, and then gently fold in the egg whites.

Ladle the batter into the waffle iron and bake until the indicator light tells you the waffles are done. Lavish with all the adornments—sweet butter, maple syrup, and/or fresh berries—and serve. Makes 8 medium waffles, depending on the size of your iron.

# Duel *of the* Gruel

The most enduring legacy of America's Civil War has very little to do with ideologies of freedom and unity. No, its aftereffect is more pervasive than that: Draw the line between the Yankee North and Rebel South, get out your breakfast bowls, and prepare to duel!

You tell me where you live, and I'll tell you what you eat. If your bowls were filled north of the Mason-Dixon line—Minnesota, Pennsylvania, Ohio—you grew up on the sacred grains of Cream of Wheat™. But if you hail anywhere south of the hills of Tennessee, you are a true grit gent through and through.

Arm your bowls and take up your spoons, gentlemen, and prepare to choose a winning recipe. I'm fairly certain if y'all whipped up a batch of Yankee Cream of Wheat and top it with a whopping dollop of vanilla Häagen-Dazs™, all your southern taste buds would be seduced and conquered. However, up against this fantastic grit recipe, it might be a draw.

> *I will ride a few hundred miles before breakfast just to be*
> *at a truck stop that serves grits. Try them; you may find*
> *your motorcycle tends to head south in the morning.*
>
> —Biker Billy, *Biker Billy Cooks with Fire*

# *Falls Mill Uptown Cheese Grits*

1 cup Falls Mill™ stone-ground grits
4 cups water, divided
¼ cup onion, finely chopped
2 tablespoons butter

2 teaspoons instant chicken bouillon
¼ cup half-and-half
2 to 4 ounces of Havarti cheese,
    coarsely grated

Place grits in a bowl and cover with 2 cups of water. Stir the grits so that light bran and chaff will rise to the top. Skim this off and set aside.

Bring 2 cups of water, the onion, butter, and instant chicken bouillon to a boil in a heavy-bottomed saucepan.

Pour the water and remaining chaff and bran off the grits in the bowl that was set aside and add them to the boiling mixture. Reduce heat to low and cook, covered, for about 20 minutes, stirring occasionally until grits soften.

Add half-and-half and cheese and stir until cheese melts and the grits are thick and creamy. Serve hot. Makes 4 half-cup servings.

## THE INSIDE LINE

If you're an aspiring grits connoisseur, use only the best—no Yankee super-market instant stuff. The best I've found are stone-ground, whole grain grits from Falls Mill, Tennessee. For more information on how to get your grits and stock up on stone-ground corn meals, flours, and a multigrain pancake mix that can't be beat, see page 211 of the Red Letter Resources at the end of this book.

## WHERE CAN I ORDER A CHICKEN-FRIED STEAK?

We all know that the thrill of eating an authentic chicken-fried steak—that funky southern cousin to Salisbury steak or Swiss steak—is inseparable from the fun of going out to your favorite eatin' place, ordering it, *waiting* for it, and having it *served* to you, hot, hot, hot on a huge plate of grits with white gravy. I'd have to open a restaurant to make *that* recipe work. So my search continues for the best chicken-fried steak in the world. I hear Threadgill's in Austin, Texas, sizzles up a good one. All of you CFS lovers out there, my address is in the back of the book. I'll wait to hear from you before I order or print a recipe.

# The Incredible, Edible Omelet

Simply put, an omelet is beaten eggs cooked in a pan and then rolled or folded, often with a filling. Men have enjoyed this refined version of scrambled eggs ever since the first omelet, a honey omelet or *ovemele,* was whipped up one morning in ancient Rome. Duke Ellington, the royal man of jazz, claimed he was the "world's greatest cooker of eggs" and also swore by the stimulating nature of caviar. Just imagine . . . a caviar omelet. Nice.

So effortless is the French, or plain, omelet to make that Howard Helmer, the American Egg Board's Senior National Representative and holder of the Guinness World Record (427 plain omelets made in 30 minutes!), can create a filled omelet in less than 40 seconds. So man your "omelet station" and choose your filling; the possibilities are endless, limited only by your imagination and refrigerator contents. The timer is on—Go!

> *Part of the secret of success in life is to eat what you like*
> *and let the food fight it out inside.*
>
> —Mark Twain

# E*ffortless* O*melet*

2 large eggs, room temperature
(organic eggs make all the
difference)
1 tablespoon lukewarm water

⅛ teaspoon salt
Dash of pepper, if desired
Butter or cooking spray

In a small bowl, beat the eggs, water, and salt together until blended. Add a dash of pepper if desired.

Heat 1 teaspoon of butter (or use cooking spray) in a 7- to 10-inch nonstick omelet pan or skillet over medium-high heat (the pan is hot and "ready" when a drop of water sizzles in it). Pour in egg mixture. (Mixture should set immediately at edges.)

With an inverted Teflon™ pancake turner, carefully push the cooked portions at the edges of the omelet toward the center so the uncooked portions can "spill over" and reach the hot surface of the pan. Tilt pan to spread the uncooked portions of the egg mixture as necessary.

When the top of the omelet is thickened and no visible liquid egg remains, fill it with your filling of choice, if any (for suggestions, see The Inside Line on next page). With the pancake turner, fold omelet in half. Let the omelet cook in the pan for 30 seconds to a minute more. Invert it onto a plate with a quick flip of the wrist or take the mellow route and simply slide it onto a plate. Makes 1 incredible omelet.

## THE INSIDE LINE

Omelets cook so quickly that the filling should be selected and prepared before starting the eggs. My friend Michael Shapiro, a.k.a. Doc Omelet, suggests trying a "whatever's in the fridge" omelet or one of the international or custom combos below:

**The Greek:** Olives, feta cheese, spinach, and onions

**The Mexican:** Salsa, onions, chiles, avocado, sausage or bacon

**The Jewish:** Kosher salami, cheddar cheese, and onions

**The Italian:** Italian sausage, pepperoni, mozzarella cheese, and onions

**The Garbage:** Anything . . . broccoli, onions, sprouts, carrots

**The Duke:** Caviar

## EGGHEAD EGGSCHANGE

What came first? Scrambled eggs or coddled eggs? Sunny-side up or eggs over easy? Huevos rancheros or a Denver omelet? Do you ever feel the urge for a "man on an island" (egg cooked in carved out toast) or crave an "Adam and Eve on a raft" (two eggs on toast)? Have you tried a Scotch woodcock—eggs served on toast with anchovies?

That little egg, the primal source of life, has cracked the code of our cuisine and our vocabulary.

You've been taught to never put all of your "eggs in one basket" for fear of "laying a big egg" in public. If you have a friend who's an "eggshell blonde" (bald), you could "egg him on" to buy an "egg-boiler" (a bowler hat). But if he is a "good egg," he'll just dismiss you as an "egghead" (intellectual) and go enjoy his egg rolls and egg cream soda (even if there are no eggs in either of them . . . ).

31

# In the Style of a Real Man

The French often baptize culinary creations with the preface *à la*—which literally means "of the" or more specifically "in the style of"—followed by the person, foods, or conditions that inspired the dish. Though today many men wear the chef's hat in the family, the following list makes it obvious who was in the kitchen working on the recipes when these phrases first came on the scene.

*à la boulangère*  In the style of the baker's wife; served with fried onions and potatoes

*à la fermière*  In the farmer's wife's style; usually a roast served with celery, carrots, turnips, and onions

*à la financière*  In the style of the banker's wife; garnished with olives, mushrooms, and cucumbers with a truffle sauce and creamed goose liver soup

*à la maréchale*  In the style of the marshal's wife; scallops or chicken breasts dipped in egg and bread crumbs and fried in butter

*à l'ambassadrice*  In the ambassador's wife's style; special sauce made with Madeira wine and veal gravy

In this new culinary Renaissance age of men in the kitchen, I add:

*au vrai homme*  In the style of a real man

As food historian Andrew F. Smith explained, "Real men do eat quiche, but it's usually only with a real woman."

# *Quiche des* **Vrais** **Hommes**

### (Real Men's Quiche)

1 prebaked 9-inch pie shell (see page 208 for the recipe)

**Quiche Filling**

2 to 3 slices of premium bacon
1 tablespoon olive oil
2 teaspoons brown sugar
6 ounces fresh salmon, cut into small chunks
4 to 5 artichoke hearts, chopped
4 to 5 mushrooms, sliced
2 tablespoons sweet red onion, finely chopped
1 clove garlic, finely chopped

1 medium tomato, seeded and diced
1 tablespoon white wine or apple juice
½ teaspoon *herbes de Provence*
¼ teaspoon paprika
5 large eggs (fresh and organic is the key!)
1 cup half-and-half
⅛ teaspoon salt
Dash of white pepper
4 to 5 drops Tabasco™, to your liking
1 cup Swiss or Monterey Jack cheese, grated
Paprika garnish

---

Bake the pie crust for 7 to 9 minutes at 400°F (see The Inside Line on prebaking a crust, page 206).

In the meanwhile, prepare the filling. In a medium pan, fry bacon until crisp. Drain the grease from the pan and pat bacon with a paper towel to remove excess oil. Crumble the bacon and set aside.

In a large skillet, heat olive oil and brown sugar over medium heat, then sauté the salmon, chopped artichoke hearts, mushrooms, onion, and garlic for 2 to 3 minutes. Add the tomato, white wine or juice, *herbes de Provence,* and paprika and sauté for a few more minutes until the flavors meld. Remove from heat and set aside.

Reset the oven temperature to 325°F. In an ample bowl, whisk together eggs, half-and-half, salt, pepper, and Tabasco. Spread the salmon-artichoke mixture over the prepared pie crust. Sprinkle with bacon pieces and cheese and pour the egg mixture over everything. Garnish with a few shakes of paprika.

Bake in the lower half of the oven for 40 to 45 minutes, until egg mixture is set. (Cover edges of pie with foil if they begin to darken.) Let cool 15 minutes before serving. Makes 6 real servings for 6 real men.

*Here's to me, and here's to you,*
*And here's to love and laughter.*
*I'll be true as long as you,*
*And not one moment after.*

—Irish breakfast toast

# Warming Up His
# Appetite

What love is to the heart, appetite is to the stomach. The stomach is the conductor that leads and livens up the great orchestra of our emotions. —Gioacchino Rossini, composer

*Scrumptious Soups, Salads, and Grand Sandwiches*

HE LOVES . . .

**H**amburger soup.—*John Elway, Denver Bronco football great*

**C**hicken soup with kreplach, as a cure above all . . . similarly, borscht, hot, for winter evenings.—*Jeffrey, Illinois*

**C**arrot soup with warm French bread and butter.—*Robert, England*

**G**reek salad and corn on the cob.—*Bob, California*

**A** Philly Cheesesteak and your apple pie.—*Tim, California*

**S**mooth peanut butter and honey sandwiches made with toasted wheat bread, served with a glass of cold milk.—*Buddy, Colorado*

# A Super Bowl of Soup

Having known and loved athletes most of my life, I am forever fasci-
nated at what—and how much!—these men ingest to fuel the ma-
chines they call "bodies." Prove me wrong, but I have yet to meet a
total vegetarian who holds a national title in this country; these guys
like their protein and lots of it.

If his Hamburger Soup was one of his secrets to bolstering his
sword arm and leading his team to two Super Bowl World Champi-
onships, I hope John Elway left the recipe with the Broncos. What
was responsible for keeping this guy's unfettered charisma ignited
throughout his career anyway? If he ate his way to becoming the
NFL's all-time winningest starting quarterback, NFL's Most Valuable
Player in 1987, and EDGE NFL Man of the Year, what *was* on his
plate . . . or in his bowl?

Now that John is "retired," I'm sure he's still stocking up on favorite fuel foods to bolster his golf game and keep the ideas flowing
for his future field of dreams. Here is the recipe, from the man himself, for that favorite soup that John and Janet Elway and their children enjoy quite often. Touchdown!

# John Elway's Hamburger Soup

2 tablespoons butter

2 medium onions, chopped

2 to 3 pounds ground beef (chuck,
   round, or sirloin; your choice)

1 garlic clove, minced

Three 15-ounce cans beef broth

One 15-ounce can tomato sauce

One 10-ounce can Rotel™ diced
   tomatoes and chile peppers

1 cup potatoes, diced with skins

1 cup carrots, peeled and diced

1 cup celery, diced

One 15-ounce can French-style
   beans

1 cup dry red wine

1 tablespoon dried parsley flakes

½ teaspoon dried basil

Salt and pepper to taste

---

In a large pot, sauté the onions and garlic in butter. Simultaneously, fry the ground meat in a large skillet until browned; drain the grease.

Add the cooked meat to the onions and garlic and sauté for a few minutes. Add all other ingredients to the pot and bring to a boil over medium heat. Reduce heat to low and simmer until the vegetables are tender (approximately 30 minutes). Season with salt and pepper. Serve with warm bread.

## *Forget Filet Mignon and Lobster....* Bring the **Chili!**

If there were a Top 10 list for the foods that men love, the word *chili* would be emblazoned nearly at the top, right under steak, lamb chops, and lemon meringue pie. Letters flood my mailbox from men who love chili.

Craig Claiborne, culinary king, cookbook author, food editor, critic for the *New York Times,* and a man who could have any dish he dreamed of served to him in a heartbeat, loved chili con carne and Häagen-Dazs™ ice cream. Jack Smith of the *L.A. Times* and his buddy, *San Francisco Chronicle*'s columnist Herb Caen used to try to impress each other with local *haute cuisine* from their respective cities and then write dueling columns about their food experiences. Herb's favorite? Dennison's™ chile con carne warmed on the stove in the can and served with a cold Mexican beer.

Chili of Champions is a winning combo of my own recipe in the book *Goddess in the Kitchen;* Expressed Chili is a fired-up rendition from my cousin-in-law, Bruce Miller. His has hip ingredients, like espresso coffee, but when it called for flat beer, I overruled. I say crack open your favorite beer, enjoy a sip, and pour the rest in!

*Chili's a lot like sex: When it's good, it's great,*
*and even when it's bad, it's not so bad.*

—Bill Boldenweck

# Chili of Champions

2 pounds premium ground beef
1 to 2 tablespoons olive oil
1½ teaspoons ground cinnamon
1 pound sirloin steak, cut into 1-inch
  cubes
⅓ cup brown sugar
4 to 6 garlic cloves, chopped
⅓ cup strong coffee (espresso is best)
1 large onion, chopped
2 stalks celery, chopped
1 green pepper, chopped
1 red pepper, chopped
2 jalapeño peppers, seeded and
  finely chopped
½ cup mushrooms, chopped
One 4-ounce can diced green chiles
3 tablespoons chili powder
1 tablespoon ground cumin

2 teaspoons dried oregano leaves
1½ teaspoons salt
1 teaspoon white pepper
Two 28-ounce cans tomatoes,
  chopped with juice
One 15-ounce can tomato sauce
1 can or bottle of beer
⅛ teaspoon baking soda
1 pound cannellini (white kidney
  beans), soaked overnight and
  drained, or two 15-ounce cans
  of your favorite beans
One 15¼-ounce can whole kernel
  corn, drained (optional)
Tabasco, salt, and more spices as
  you wish
Chopped onions, grated cheese, and
  sour cream garnishes (optional)

---

In a large Dutch oven or heavy-bottomed pot, brown the ground beef over medium-high heat. Drain the grease.

Add the olive oil, cinnamon, cubed steak, brown sugar, garlic, coffee, and onions

39

and sauté for about 5 minutes, stirring occasionally to keep the bottom from burning. Reduce heat to medium and add the celery, all three types of peppers, mushrooms, chiles, and spices, and simmer for 10 to 15 minutes until everything starts to smell really good.

Reduce the heat to low and add the tomatoes, tomato sauce, and beer; cook for a few minutes. Stir in the baking soda (the chili will bubble and boil for a few seconds). When it's done acting up, add beans and simmer uncovered for 1½ to 2 hours or until beans are thoroughly cooked. (*Note:* If you are using cooked, canned beans, add them *after* the chili has cooked for about 1½ hours.) Add the corn if desired.

Tune up the chili with Tabasco, salt, and more spices to suit your taste. Serve with favorite garnishes like onions, grated cheese, and sour cream, and be sure to have some crackers, corn bread (see recipe on page 16), and rivers of ice-cold beer on hand. Makes 6 to 8 servings.

---

### HE MUST HAVE BEEN STEWED

In the early twentieth century, chef Auguste Escoffier, one of the most prolific chefs to ever oversee a soup, declared that a proper consommé has not only meat in the broth but at least sixteen vegetables as well (although most countries other than France used approximately six).

I guess that dismisses his own country's darling, *Gratinée Lyonnaise,* otherwise known as French onion soup; one lowly onion simmers in that pot.

# Spooning Up Memories of JFK's Soup

I've decided, after interviewing hundreds of gastronomes, that guys who grew up cither in cold climates or near seaboards, lakes, streams, or even trout ponds are more passionate about eating soup than are hot-house, land-locked gentlemen. It's a whimsical theory, but I do know that Mike Love of the Beach Boys, who grew up in Surf City USA, favors sumptuous homemade soups over most other entrées!

Born and bred in New England, near Cape Cod, President John F. Kennedy loved the sea and any connection to it. It is no surprise that he loved seafood, particularly a hearty New England fish chowder that he would request several days *in a row* while at the White House. In fact, in 1961, First Lady Jacqueline submitted a recipe for the fish chowder to the *Congressional Club Cook Book,* which is still in print today. If clams and oysters and seafood be the foods of love, Kennedy was smitten. In honor of a true chowder man, I offer my best recipe.

*An empty stomach*
*is not a good political advisor.*

—Albert Einstein

# Noble New England Clam Chowder

### A favorite of President John F. Kennedy

1¼ pounds (3 to 4 medium) potatoes, diced into ½-inch pieces and par-boiled

4 cups half-and-half

3 cups whole milk

2 teaspoons minced garlic

2 tablespoons clam base (found in specialty food stores)

2 teaspoons sugar

½ cup flour

¼ cup butter, melted

Three 6½-ounce cans chopped clams, drained; juice reserved

Salt and pepper to taste

Fresh chives, chopped

---

Dice and parboil potatoes until *al dente*.

Using a large *bain-marie* or double-boiler, heat to a hot simmer the half-and-half, milk, garlic, clam base (see The Inside Line on next page for a substitution), clam juice (strained from the can), and sugar.

In a small bowl, combine flour and butter to form a roux. Add about ½ cup of the chowder concoction to the roux, blend well, and then whisk the roux into the large pot. Cook for 10 to 15 minutes until the chowder begins to thicken. Add the clams and potatoes and simmer for another 10 to 12 minutes until the potatoes are tender (but take care not to *overcook* the potatoes).

Season with salt and pepper and garnish each serving with fresh chives. Makes 4 servings, fit for a true New Englander and president.

**THE INSIDE LINE**

Clam base can be found in most specialty food stores. However, to make a homemade clam base, simply puree the contents of a 6½-ounce can of clams with 1 tablespoon salt and 2 teaspoons lemon juice; use 2 tablespoons of this base for the recipe.

*May the saddest day of your future be no worse
Than the happiest day of your past.*

—Irish proverb

## It All Started with Chicken Soup

Chicken soup has the power to cure colds and cold hearts. It is our birthright to slurp the golden broth when its magic is needed to soothe the soul and comfort the senses. Mm . . . Mm . . . good. . . .

Tom Lagana, the author who cooked up *Chicken Soup for the Prisoner's Soul,* another serving from the "Chicken Soup for the Soul" series, sent me his story and favorite recipe:

> Do you know what I eat for breakfast? Chicken soup. As a little boy I hated breakfast foods and simply refused to eat. When I started kindergarten, my mom finally stumbled on to something I would eat for breakfast. The tradition has continued into my adult life.

In light of her father's love for her soup, in *Newman's Own Cookbook* Nell Newman says of dad Paul, "Give my father a hearty soup, a can of beer, and a bag of popcorn, and he is as close to heaven as he can get. He does handstands over my chicken soup." I have never known a wise man to turn down something made with love. So get out your spoons and enjoy this simple version of a heartwarming, immune-boosting staple.

# Tom Lagana's Original Chicken Soul Soup

3-pound whole fryer chicken
6 to 8 cups water
1 garlic clove, diced
1 cup onion, diced
1 cup celery, diced

½ cup carrots, diced
½ cup leeks, chopped
3 tablespoons fresh parsley, chopped
Freshly ground black pepper (salt optional)

---

Rinse the chicken and remove excess fat. Place the chicken in large Dutch oven, add the vegetables, and add enough water to cover the chicken. Bring to a boil over medium-high heat.

Reduce heat to low and simmer, covered, for 90 minutes. Remove from the heat and remove the chicken. (You may debone the chicken and return the meat to the soup if you wish.) Serve steaming hot, garnished with parsley and ground pepper. Serves 6.

*My soul is satisfied as with a rich feast.*

—Psalms 63:5

# All Dressed Up *and* Ready to Go

Move over Paul Newman, The Madge has arrived. Blender in hand, he is ready to give you a *whirr* for your money. Not to say Newman's Own™ salad dressings are shabby—far from it; they are the best you can buy. In the introduction to *Newman's Own Cookbook,* the tale is told:

> For years, Paul Newman and his longtime buddy A. E. Hotchner filled old wine bottles with their homemade salad dressing to give to friends as Christmas gifts. . . . A smashing success, Newman's Own products have generated more than $100 million in after-tax profits, all of which have been donated to charitable and educational causes.

Every cent.

The Madge, a.k.a. former pizza baron and self-styled kitchen god Mark Englund, has promised to give me all after-tax profits of every recipe of Madge's Own I make and give away. What a scam! I'll never see a cent, but the dressing, which can be used in place of (and I quote) "any cheap old salad dressing," tastes priceless.

# $\mathcal{M}$adge's Own Salad Dressing

2 cups red wine vinegar
1 cup extra-virgin olive oil
¼ cup warm water
1½ teaspoons Dijon mustard
1½ teaspoons sugar
1½ teaspoons garlic, minced
1 tablespoon honey

1 tablespoon fresh parsley, finely
  chopped
1 tablespoon green onion, minced
1 teaspoon dried basil
1 teaspoon salt
1 teaspoon ground black pepper

Put all ingredients into a blender or food processor and torch! Makes a bit more than a bottle of Newman's Own. Adorn your favorite salad and enjoy!

*Some people have sexual dreams,*
*but I dream about salad.*

—Paul Newman, *Newman's Own Cookbook*

# Give 'Em a **Helluva Salad,** Oscar

Why certain foods hit the superlotto taste bud jackpot in some men and barely affect, if not deflect, others is a perpetually unfolding mystery. Tastes developed from what your momma made, what your childhood feel-good favorites were, and what you used to live on (like tuna fish salad-potato chip sandwiches) when you first left home.

Did you grow up in a northern climate, southern atmosphere, or in another culture altogether, like New Orleans? What regional, ethnic, or local influences were sprinkled into your meals? One man may dream of hot hushpuppies and their toasty taste, while another gets wistful when he thinks of that apple pie his old girlfriend used to bake.

An all-time favorite of President Harry Truman was Waldorf salad. The original Waldorf, a blend of apples, celery, and mayonnaise, was dreamed up in 1893 by the Waldorf-Astoria Hotel's *maître d'hôtel,* Oscar Tschirky, a.k.a. Oscar of the Waldorf. As time passed, cooks "tainted" the original recipe with all sorts of improvisations—walnuts, raisins, pecans, and grapes. This is truly a salad worth tasting, but may Oscar forgive me. . . . I messed with it even more. What the hell, the buck stops here.

*If you can't stand the heat, get out of the kitchen.*

—Harry Truman

48

# With-It Waldorf Salad

A favorite of President Harry Truman

2 teaspoons olive oil
½ pound cooked turkey, cubed
¾ teaspoon Madras curry powder
3 large, crisp apples, cored and diced
Juice from a wedge of lemon
4 medium stalks celery, diced
1 cup chopped pecans, lightly
  toasted
½ cup white raisins

¾ cup mayonnaise (Hellmann's™
  or Best Foods™, the only kind)
⅛ teaspoon nutmeg
⅛ teaspoon ground white pepper
Salt to taste
1 small head Boston lettuce, washed
  and dried
Fresh parsley sprigs
Pecan halves, lightly toasted

---

Heat olive oil over medium-high heat in a large skillet. Sprinkle curry powder over the turkey and sear in the hot oil for a minute or two. Set aside. In the meanwhile, place all the pecans (separate the halves from the pieces) on a baking sheet and toast in the oven under the broiler for a few minutes, until golden.

Place the apples in a large bowl and sprinkle with lemon juice. Fold in celery, chopped pecans, and raisins. Spoon the mayonnaise over this mixture and sprinkle with nutmeg, pepper, and salt; fold in. Add the seared turkey pieces and toss lightly. Refrigerate the salad mixture for 1 hour.

Arrange lettuce on salad plates and spoon the salad onto the lettuce. Garnish with parsley and pecans. Serve immediately. Makes 4 servings.

# Hail to the Caesar

Upon what meat doth this our Caesar feed,
That he is grown so great? —**Shakespeare,** *Julius Caesar*

I know, I know. The first Caesar salad had nothing to do with the great Roman emperor (although I still like the idea of Cleopatra, queen-of-Egypt-and-goddess-by-proxy, conquering Caesar's heart and empire by simply purring, "If you give me your armies and their general, I'll make you a killer Caesar salad").

This hands-down all-time men's favorite superstar salad was tossed by a man—an Italian man, Caesar Cardini—for a man—his brother Alex, a visiting Italian Air Force veteran—in Tijuana, Mexico, at a Fourth of July party for a bunch of men way back when in 1924. This great Caesar quickly threw some in-house foodstuff together and presented it to the party as the Aviator Salad. Brother Alex called it "Caesar's."

Considering the quote, it probably wasn't meat at all that grew Caesar so great, but grilled portabello mushrooms, which pack a great protein punch. And remember, the secret to making a kick-ass Caesar is to always mix the dressing in the bowl.

*The Creator while forcing men to eat in order to live,*
*tempts him to do so with appetite and*
*then rewards him with pleasure.*

—Brillat-Savarin

# $\mathcal{P}$*ortabello* **C***aesar* **S***alad*

3 to 4 large portabello mushrooms, caps sliced into ¼-inch pieces, grilled

4 to 6 anchovy fillets

1 heaping tablespoon garlic (4 to 6 cloves), finely minced

2 tablespoons Dijon mustard

Juice from 1 lemon

2 egg yolks

⅔ cup extra-virgin olive oil

½ teaspoon kosher salt

½ teaspoon freshly ground black pepper

¾ cup Parmesan cheese, freshly grated, divided

2 heads romaine lettuce, washed and patted dry

½ small sweet red onion, cut into thinly sliced rings (optional)

Croutons (optional)

Additional anchovies

---

To prepare the portabellos, coat them with Madge's Own Salad Dressing (recipe on page 47) or a bit of seasoned olive oil and grill, broil, or sauté them for 3 to 4 minutes per side. Set aside.

Mash the anchovies and garlic together in a large wooden salad bowl with a fork. Add the mustard and blend. Whisk in the lemon juice and egg yolk, followed by the olive oil; whisk well until blended.

Blend in salt and pepper and about half of the cheese. Add the romaine lettuce and toss until each leaf is well coated. Arrange on a chilled platter, top with the grilled portabellos, and sprinkle with the remaining cheese. Garnish with sliced onion rings, homemade garlic croutons, and another anchovy fillet if you feel the urge. Makes 4 noble Caesars.

# Not Too Sloppy to Get in the **Mood**

Cookbook author and "Diet Queen of DeWitt" JoAnna M. Lund doesn't mince words—and doesn't waste her time mincing garlic or onions, for that matter. She's too busy enjoying the rewards of living a healthy life with her "truck-drivin' man," husband Cliff. If you want healthy, easy-to-make food that tastes as good as it looks *and* meets her final "must"—can be made from ingredients found in DeWitt, Iowa—pick up a copy of *Cooking Healthy with a Man in Mind*.

When JoAnna shared this recipe, she wrote, "I think it's perfect for your book," and continued with a spunky tale of a woman who made her Healthy JO's for a "meat and potatoes through and through" hubby who needed to lower his cholesterol. JoAnna added, "Her husband raved and raved—even helped her with the dishes—and told her that they were the next best thing to making love! Now, whenever I'm at a book signing and share that story, a man in the group almost always asks, 'And where did you get that cookbook?'" Here's to Jo's!

## **H**ealthy *JO's*

| | |
|---|---|
| 1 pound extra-lean ground turkey or beef | ½ cup chunky salsa, your favorite brand |
| ½ cup finely chopped onion | 1 tablespoon Brown Sugar Twin™ |
| One 8-ounce can (1 cup) tomato sauce | 6 reduced-calorie hamburger buns |

In a large skillet sprayed with olive oil–flavored cooking spray, brown the meat and onion. Add the tomato sauce, salsa, and Brown Sugar Twin. Mix well to combine. Lower heat and simmer for 15 minutes, stirring occasionally.

For each sandwich, spoon ⅓ cup of the meat filling between hamburger buns. Makes 6 servings.

## THE  INSIDE  LINE

Of course you can grab some sesame-topped Kaiser rolls and use real brown sugar in place of substitute sugar. Since JoAnna has tamed the beastly fat in this super Sloppy Joe, you'll be forgiven the few extra calories.

### INSIDE DISH FIT FOR A KING

I knew it. After all this time, you are still intrigued with the King of Crooners and what favorite foods soothed his soul. We've all heard about his beloved peanut butter and banana sandwiches, but if you can't live without a recipe for Elvis' favorite fried dill pickles, six-egg omelet with burnt bacon, or Miss Vertie's sweet potato pie, why not add an Elvis cookbook to your library:

*Are You Hungry Tonight?: Elvis' Favorite Recipes*

*Fit for a King: The Elvis Presley Cookbook*

*The Presley Family and Friends Cookbook: A Cookbook and Memory Book from Those Who Knew Elvis Best*

*The Life and Cuisine of Elvis Presley*

*The I Love Elvis Cookbook*

# Let Them Eat **Red's Hot Dogs**

First Lady Eleanor Roosevelt, who was a casual entertainer during her White House tenure, preferred channeling her energy into championing her many causes—none of which was the pursuit of culinary expertise. In fact, at a private luncheon for King George VI and his Queen, Elizabeth, the Roosevelts served hot dogs and baked beans. Surprisingly, the King was amused and enjoyed his dog.

Nathan's Famous™ or Hebrew Nationals™—if you love 'em, you truly love 'em. On Chicago's far South Side, near the corner of 111th and Western, resides an American institution known as Red's Hot Dogs, a half-a-century-old business success that grew from a hot dog cart to a shack to its present empire.

The following *pièce de resistance,* recreated by Charlie Girsch, a Chicago homeboy now living Red's Hot Dog–less in Minnesota, is Red's famous Chicago-style hot dog without the benefit of Red or Vienna™ Hot Dogs or a bun steamer. Charlie claims the secret lies in "soggy buns and celery salt."

## **U**nreal **R**ed's **H**ot **D**ogs

2 of your favorite off-the-shelf hot dogs

2 of your favorite white bread hot dog buns

Ketchup, mustard, relish, onions, tomatoes, celery salt, ground black pepper, and a hot pepper or two if you can stand the heat

Simmer the hot dogs in water in a large saucepan (that can accommodate a colander). When the color is cooked out, nestle the colander in the saucepan above the water to catch the rising steam.

Place the separated buns face down in the colander. Cover it with a lid and let the steam caress the buns for a minute or two. (You might lose a bun or two to the super-sogs while perfecting your bun-warming technique, but persist.)

Deposit the hot dog carefully in the warmed bun and slather on the condiments. Before you take that first bite, shake celery salt all over it, maybe a sprinkle of ground pepper, and run it through the garden!

---

**THIS LITTLE PIGGY GOT MUNCHED**

The late, great Jerry Garcia, the cosmic godfather and lead guitarist for the Grateful Dead, loved his junk food. Give him a tune to sing and a pig in a blanket and he was as happy as a pig in . . . well, let's say "paradise."

Jerry liked little hot dogs bun- dled in a biscuit, but *piggies en couchage* can be any "little" food swathed and cooked in another, like oysters or cube steak in bacon. The Brits, however, prefer their "toads in a hole," link sausages wrapped in Yorkshire pudding. Jerry would have loved toads too.

# Mr. Crunchy *Meets the* Big Cheese

"Only in America," you think, "would a man say he loves something as common as a grilled cheese sandwich." My thoughts exactly, until I started asking men if they ever ate a Monte Cristo, which is basically a flamboyant grilled cheese. This triple-decker whopper of Swiss cheese and baked ham is dipped in egg batter and sometimes grilled, but more classically, deep fried, and topped with powdered sugar and served with red currant jelly and fruit compote. Oh my.

But wait, they love 'em in France too! The rumor is they originated on Monte Cristo (remember the "Count of . . ."?). Who knows? The French, however, hail them as *Croque-Monsieur,* literally translated, "Mr. Crunchy." Imagine this: If you take the same sandwich, add a little turkey or chicken, and nestle two round, sunny-side eggs on top of it, it is instantly transformed into a *Croque-Madame. Vive la différence!*

Popularized at Disneyland's Blue Bayou restaurant, this version of the "Disneyland Sandwich" is my offering to you. And for all of you die-hard grilled-cheese sandwich loyalists and eager pan masters out there, a sensational grilled-cheese stunner follows.

# $\mathscr{M}$onte Cristo Disneyland Sandwich

| Batter | Sandwiches |
|---|---|
| 2 large eggs | 6 slices white bread |
| ½ cup milk | Four 1-ounce slices Swiss cheese |
| ¼ teaspoon ground cinnamon | Two 1-ounce slices premium deli ham |
| ¼ teaspoon salt | Two 1-ounce slices turkey |
| ½ cup unbleached flour | Confectioners' sugar and marmalade |
| 1 teaspoon baking powder | garnish |

To make the batter, whisk together in a deep bowl the eggs, milk, cinnamon, and salt. Add the flour and baking powder and mix until smooth. Chill while you assemble the sandwiches.

To assemble the sandwich, layer (in order) a slice of bread, ham, cheese, bread, turkey, cheese, and another slice of bread. Secure sandwiches with toothpicks (snap the top of the toothpick so it is flush with the bread) and cut sandwich on the diagonal or into quarters.

You have two options for cooking: Heat a sandwich grill (like George Foreman's Mean Lean Grilling Machine™) to medium-high and coat with butter. Dip the sandwiches on both sides in the batter and grill for 3 to 4 minutes until golden and crispy.

Or, to cook the Cristo the classic way, heat about 4 inches of vegetable oil in a deep fryer to 360°F. Fry the sandwiches in oil for 3 to 4 minutes until golden brown, turning if necessary.

Remove the toothpicks and dust with confectioners' sugar before serving with marmalade or jelly. (Barbara's Jalapeño Jelly on page 17 makes a great match.) Makes 2 *Croque-Monsieur à la Disneyland.*

# *B*ig *C*heese *G*rilled *G*rande

4 to 6 large red onion rings
1 tablespoon sherry
3 ounces sharp cheddar cheese
3 ounces Emmenthaler Swiss
  cheese
1 ounce feta cheese

½ apple, cored and thinly sliced into
  disks
4 large slices honey-nut wheat bread,
  buttered on one side
Dijon mustard
Sprinkle of dried dill

---

In a large pan, sauté the sliced onion rings in sherry. Remove from pan and set aside, leaving the pan "seasoned." Grate the cheddar and Emmenthaler cheeses and crumble the feta.

Assemble two sandwiches by placing two slices of bread, buttered side down, on a small cutting board or plate, topped with cheeses, sliced apple disks, a sprinkle of dried dill, a little more cheese, and the top pieces of bread anointed with mustard, buttered side up.

Preferably microwave the sandwiches for 20 seconds (the cheeses need a jump-start for a proper melt-down). Move sandwiches to the large pan and grill each side over medium heat until golden brown (about 2½ minutes per side), until the cheese is oozing out of the sides of the sandwich. Eat. Makes 2 awesome grilled-cheese sandwiches.

## THE PHILADELPHIA STORY

If you haven't been to Philadelphia, you've never had a Philly Cheesesteak—plain and simple. It doesn't seem fair that Philly natives can order up a national treasure at practically any street corner, while the rest of us can only daydream about eating an authentic Philly Cheesesteak (though some joints actually crank out honorable cheesesteak clones).

What makes this masterpiece of shaved roasted beef rib-eye, sizzled and tossed with yellow onions on big stainless steel grills, slapped in an Italian roll, topped with green peppers, and melded together with warm, gooey white American or provolone cheese so great? Some cheesesteak aficionados say it's the bread.

The rest of the country has its subs (it's the shape), grinders (it's the meatballs), heroes (it's the size), hoagies (who knows?), and Carnegie Deli's pastrami sandwiches (we all know). The knockout New Orleans *muffeleta* and Mardi Gras po' boys with their dandy fillings and badass bread can sway a hungry man's heart most any day. But, back to the Philly. . . . Small or large? Sauce or onions? Here or to go?

*A little nonsense now and then*
*is relished by the wisest man.*

—Anonymous

59

# It's Something *in the* Air

I used to take cooking classes when I was younger . . .
because girls weren't interested in me and I thought
I may be alone for the rest of my life.
—**Michael Jordan**

We can all rest assured that Michael Jordan doesn't need to worry about the girls anymore. Consequently, the legendary Lord of the Court has turned his attentions from basketball and cooking classes to more majestic ventures. His Airness has taken to taste-testing his favorite foods and taking them to the hoop at trademark restaurants, including Michael Jordan's 23 in Chapel Hill, North Carolina.

With star chef Andrew Williams heating up the food court, Team Jordan is cooking up a slam-dunk recipe for success. The Peekytoe Crab Sandwich, which dazzled The Man's taste buds, is gracing the menu at 23. Fun to say and divine to dine on, Peekytoes are a real treat. The cooking classes worked.

## *Michael Jordan's 23*
## *Peekytoe Crab Sandwich*

1½ tablespoons sour cream

1½ tablespoons mayonnaise

½ pound fresh jumbo lump crabmeat
(clean, no shells)

Zest of ½ lemon, slightly blanched in
boiling water

2 tablespoons red bell pepper,
blanched in boiling water, finely diced

½ tablespoon fresh basil chiffonade (thinly sliced strips)

1 tablespoon lemon juice, freshly squeezed

Salt and white pepper

1 large Idaho potato, peeled

Approximately ¼ cup clarified butter

---

In a small bowl, mix together the sour cream and mayonnaise. Then combine all other ingredients (except the salt, white pepper, and potato), blending lightly and taking care not to break up the crab too much. Season with salt and pepper and reserve.

Using a mandolin grater, shred the peeled potato into fine strings. Lay down 8 small beds of potato string on a clean surface. Top with 1 ounce of the crab salad per bed and complete each stack with more potato strings.

With a spatula, gently lay each bundle down in a hot sauté pan oiled with clarified butter. When the grilled side is golden (take a peek), flip the bundle over. Brown the other side until the crab bundle is heated thoroughly; lightly season with salt.

At Michael Jordan's 23, guests are served two small Peekytoe Crab Sandwiches with a small bit of field greens and a citrus butter sauce. Makes 3 to 4 servings.

### THE INSIDE LINE

To clarify the butter, simply melt it, let stand for a few minutes, skim the butterfat ("whey") from the top, and strain the clear butter (also called "ghee") into a container.

*If you want to improve your quality of life,*
*there are only two things you have to invest in:*
*Quality and life.*

—Attributed to Dorismarie Welcher,
Queen of the Hudson

# Pasta, Pizza, and
# Molto Risotto

I learned to cook because I like to eat well,
and I like to eat that way every day.

—Giuliano Hazan, *Every Night Italian*

*Man-Pleasing Meals to Fuel His Fires*

HE LOVES . . .

**B**ucatini all'amatriciana . . . and a bottle of Bruno Verdi 1996. . . .
*—Mario Batali, star chef and author*

**C**rispy sausage penne served with a bottle of Amarone, a most divine
Italian wine.*—Marco, Switzerland*

**S**callop ravioli with pistachio pesto.*—Israel, Mexico and Nevada*

**S**paghetti and meatballs, a sure winner, but I have to admit a distinct
love for one of my favorite white trash dishes, tuna noodle casserole.
*—Andrew, California*

**M**y mother's paella.*—Vicente, Spain*

# No **Limp Noodles** Here

Just admit it. If I asked you to tell me what your all-time, over-the-top favorite food was, I know more than half of you armchair epicures out there would say (though probably under your breath), "I love macaroni and cheese," or "Yum, tuna noodle casserole."

Hey, take pride and hold your forks high! Along with spaghetti and meatballs and lasagna, these two farinaceous fantasy dishes are at the top of the list of legions of eager eaters, from sport heroes and superstars to presidents and humble gastronomes. You are in great company.

Michael Jordan insists on having mac-n-cheese on the menu at his restaurant The Steak House in New York City because he "loved his mother's cheesy baked macaroni and thinks it's the ideal accompaniment to steak—at least for athletes who can burn off unlimited calories." Considering how smitten Sir Elton John was by her macaroni and cheese, singer and cookbook diva Patti LaBelle lays claim, "I don't know who turned Elton John on to soul music, but I do know who turned him on to soul food." What did Ronald Reagan have served to him in the hospital after he was shot? You guessed it: macaroni and cheese.

Ever the no-nonsense native son, President Harry Truman was most fond of his wife's all-American tuna noodle casserole, served with chocolate pudding or ice cream dessert. To my surprise, my own brother, a gourmand and man of unparalleled good taste, confessed his passion for that same pet dish, good ol' "chicken of the sea soufflé," complete with the trademark potato chips and cream of mushroom soup.

If you love it, choose to cruise. I hereby offer you the ultimate renditions of these two quintessential comfort foods.

## Majestic Macaroni and Cheese

1 pound elbow macaroni
1 tablespoon extra-virgin olive oil
8 tablespoons (1 stick) sweet butter
1 large garlic clove, minced
1½ cups whole milk, warmed
½ cup sour cream
½ cup ricotta cheese
1 tablespoon flour
½ teaspoon Worcestershire sauce
½ cup (2 ounces) Parmesan cheese, freshly grated

1 cup (4 ounces) sharp Cheddar cheese, shredded
1 cup (4 ounces) Monterey Jack cheese, shredded
1 large egg, beaten (optional)
¾ teaspoon kosher or seasoned salt
½ teaspoon freshly ground pepper
½ cup bread crumbs (preferably homemade), finely crumbled
¼ cup walnuts, finely ground
¼ to ½ cup (1 to 2 ounces) Parmesan cheese, freshly grated

Preheat the oven to 350°F. Grease a 2½-quart casserole or baking dish (oil spray works well).

Bring a large pot of lightly salted water with the olive oil to boil over high heat.

65

Add the macaroni and cook until barely *al dente*, approximately 6 to 7 minutes (do not overcook). Drain well and return the macaroni to the pot (heat off).

Melt the butter in a large saucepan over low heat. Add the garlic and sauté for 1 to 2 minutes. Then stir the melted butter and garlic into the macaroni.

In a large bowl, mix together the warmed milk, sour cream, ricotta cheese, flour, and Worcestershire sauce. In another bowl, toss together the Parmesan, sharp Cheddar, and Monterey Jack cheeses. Fold the milk mixture, the cheeses, and the egg, if using, *into* the macaroni and season with salt and pepper. Mix together gently and transfer to the casserole dish.

Mix together the bread crumbs and ground walnuts and sprinkle on top of the casserole, followed by a generous amount of grated Parmesan. Bake for 30 to 35 minutes until golden brown and bubbly. Serve hot. Makes 6 soothing servings.

## THE INSIDE LINE

In *LaBelle Cuisine,* Patti swears, "Ask anyone who makes incredible macaroni and cheese . . . I bet you that Velveeta™ will be in there." Experiment with different cheeses until you find the combination that really turns you on.

*To a man, serving him food is like offering him a breast.*

—L. M. Azar

# *Luxury* **Tuna** **Casserole**

A favorite of President Harry Truman

One 8-ounce package wide egg
    noodles or 3 cups uncooked shell
    pasta
3 tablespoons unsalted butter,
    divided
½ cup (1 to 2 stalks) celery, finely
    chopped
½ cup (1 bunch) scallions, finely
    chopped
4 to 5 mushrooms, sliced
1 to 2 tablespoons bourbon
    or sherry
2 tablespoons fresh Italian parsley,
    finely chopped
One 10¾-ounce can cream of
    mushroom soup

1 cup sour cream
¼ cup milk
1 cup tiny frozen peas
5 to 6 green olives with pimento,
    sliced (optional)
1 teaspoon *herbes de Provence*
½ teaspoon curry powder
½ teaspoon kosher salt
Freshly ground pepper
Two 6-ounce cans solid white tuna
    packed in water, drained and
    rinsed
2 cups potato chips, crushed
Parmesan cheese, freshly grated
Paprika

---

Cook the egg noodles or shell pasta in boiling water until done, according to package directions. Drain in a colander, rinsing briefly in cold water. Turn into a large mixing bowl, stir in 1 tablespoon of butter until melted, and set aside.

Melt the remaining 2 tablespoons of butter in a large sauté pan over medium heat, sautéing the celery, scallions, and mushrooms until soft. Add the bourbon or sherry and cook a minute longer. Gently fold the sauté mixture and the Italian parsley into the pasta.

Preheat the oven to 350°F. In another bowl, combine the soup, sour cream, and milk. Add the peas, sliced olives, *herbes de Provence,* curry powder, salt and pepper to taste; blend in the tuna. Gently fold this mixture *into* the bowl of noodles or shells.

Spread 1 cup of the crushed potato chips over the bottom of a buttered 2½-quart casserole or soufflé dish. Spread the tuna-noodle mixture evenly over the chips. Top with the remaining cup of crushed chips, sprinkle with Parmesan cheese, garnish with paprika, and bake for 45 minutes until golden brown. Cool for 10 minutes before serving. Makes 6 servings.

*Serve this dish with much too much wine*
*for your guests . . . and a huge salad.*
*You will be famous in about half an hour.*

—Jeff Smith, *The Frugal Gourmet*

# Never Fear, **Mario** Is Here

Virtuoso Mario Batali is a firebrand in our gastronomic universe: He defies all that is vogue and trendy and celebrates a sumptuous simplicity instead. He is a true inspiration to anyone who likes to eat or cook. After all, if a kid from Seattle, Washington—granted, one with good Italian genes—can dazzle the elite New York City culinary club with the unpretentious and bold Italian fare found at his restaurants Babbo, Lupa, and Esca, there's hope for all of us food fledglings.

Just flip through the pages of *Mario Batali Simple Italian Food* or stir up some fun with *Mario Batali Holiday Food*. You say you don't do cookbooks? Then grab your remote and indulge in food fantasies with *Molto Mario* on the TV Food Network, or nab a recipe for an awesome osso buco at *foodtv.com*. All bases covered? *Andiamo a tavola!*

What food does Mario love? I asked him what his "last meal" would be. . . . "This dish is perfect: the preparation is simple, the pasta hearty enough to carry the pork, the acidity, the sweetness, and the heat; the Pecorino adds just the right amount of saltiness. I would definitely choose this as my last meal, matched with a bottle of Bruno Verdi 1996, a Buttafuoco from Lombardia. The last meal would have to take place in July, so I could have fresh blackberries, drizzled with *aceto balsamico di Modena* for dessert." Rest in bliss, Mario.

# Mario Batali's Bucatini all'Amatriciana

| | |
|---|---|
| 6 quarts water | 1 red onion, cut in half and sliced |
| 2 tablespoons salt | 1½ teaspoons chili flakes |
| ¾ pound pancetta or guanciale (the | Salt and pepper |
| meat of a pig's jowl that has been | 2 cups basic tomato sauce (recipe |
| cured similarly to bacon, thinly sliced | follows) |
| and rendered) | 1 pound bucatini |
| 3 garlic cloves, sliced | Pecorino cheese |

Bring the water to a boil and add the salt.

In a 12- to 14-inch sauté pan, combine garlic, guanciale, onion, and chilis and sauté until onion is soft. Add tomato sauce, reduce heat, and allow to simmer 10 to 15 minutes.

Cook bucatini in the boiling water according to the package directions, until tender but still *al dente,* about 12 minutes. Remove pasta from heat, drain, and add to simmering sauce. Toss to coat and divide among 4 heated bowls. Serve immediately, topped with freshly grated Pecorino cheese. Makes 4 servings. *Fantastico!*

# Mario Batali's Basic Tomato Sauce

¼ cup extra-virgin olive oil

1 Spanish onion, chopped in ¼-inch dice

4 garlic cloves, peeled and thinly sliced

3 tablespoons fresh thyme leaves, chopped, or 1 tablespoon dried thyme

½ medium carrot, finely shredded

Two 28-ounce cans peeled whole tomatoes, crushed by hand, juices reserved

Salt to taste

In a 3-quart saucepan, heat the olive oil over medium heat. Add the onion and garlic and cook until soft and light golden brown, about 8 to 10 minutes. Add the thyme and carrot and cook 5 minutes more, until carrot is soft.

Add the tomatoes and juice and bring to a boil, stirring often. Lower the heat and simmer for 30 minutes until the consistency is "as thick as hot cereal." Season with salt and serve or use in recipe. This sauce holds for one week in the refrigerator or up to six months in the freezer. Makes 4 cups.

## DOING THE CAN-CAN

Some chefs abhor using canned ingredients in their creations; most regular Joes and home-based gourmands think cans and their contents are the greatest invention since the wheel. Viva convenience!

Who then, is to blame—or bless—for inventing the first canned food? A man. In 1794, eager to acquire more real estate through extended military and naval campaigns, Napoleon Bonaparte offered 12,000 francs to the person who perfected a method of preserving food. Fifteen years later, Nicolas Appert boiled up some meat and potatoes and vacuum-packed them in jars with corks and tar.

When this French military secret went public a year later, after being published in a book written by Appert, Englishman Peter Durand—not to be outdone by the French—refined the idea and patented a tin-plated steel container: the can.

*Italian food is all about style and good ingredients—*
*ingredients native to your village—the whole point*
*here is that Italian cooks use what is*
*available to them, and only the best of that.*

—Mario Batali, *Simple Italian Food*

# Go Ahead, **M**ake **M**y **M**usic

Some men make history, some make waves, some make love, and some make all of the above, and more. Dan Healy makes sound. If you have ever been to a Grateful Dead concert or listened to Quicksilver Messenger Service, or vintage Dave Matthews Band, very likely Dan, legendary music producer and sound engineer of the '60s, '70s, '80s, and '90s, was enhancing your mind. The guys with the instruments may have been making the music, but the man behind the curtain—the wizard of the soundboard  was making your trip over the rainbow complete with his audio magic.

While Dan's sound waves will forever resonate through space and time, he now kicks back with ladylove Patti feasting on his favorite foods, like his spaghetti with meatballs. Meanwhile, oceans away, my friend David Mogelefsky in Maui may even be listening to some Dan-built Dead on his stereo while assembling his Uncle Lou's *Lasagna Cubana*. More than a century ago, this recipe was brought from Italy through Cuba to Lou by a girl named Josephine.

It's a small world . . . and the band plays on. . . .

*Everything you see I owe to spaghetti.*

—Sophia Loren

# Dan Healy's Weapons Grade Meatballs and Spaghetti

**Weapons Grade Meatballs**
¾ cup bread crumbs (homemade are best)
½ cup milk
2 eggs
1 cup Romano cheese, finely grated
⅓ pound ground beef
⅓ pound ground veal
⅓ pound pork
2 cloves garlic, minced

2 tablespoons fresh parsley, minced
Salt and pepper
Olive oil for frying

**Sauce**
Four 15-ounce cans tomato sauce
One 14½-ounce can beef broth
Salt and pepper
1 pound spaghetti, cooked according
   to package directions

---

In a large mixing bowl, soak the bread crumbs in milk for 1 to 2 minutes. Add all other "meatball" ingredients, combine, and form golf ball–sized meatballs. Fry the meatballs in olive oil in a large skillet over medium-high heat until nicely browned.

In a large saucepan, prepare the sauce by simply combining the tomato sauce and beef broth, seasoning with salt and pepper, and simmering over medium-low heat. Gently transfer the meatballs to the tomato sauce and simmer, covered, for 45 minutes to 1 hour, until the sauce is seasoned and the meatballs are cooked as you like them.

When the meatballs are almost done, prepare the spaghetti according to package directions. Drain and add a little olive oil to keep the pasta from sticking together. Transfer the spaghetti to another pan, ladle a little of the meatball sauce over it, and keep it warm. When you're ready to feast, serve the spaghetti topped with meatballs and sauce. Makes 4 servings.

## *Lasagna* **Cubana**

1 batch Basic Tomato Sauce

One 6-ounce can tomato paste

2 tablespoons brown sugar

¾ teaspoon crushed red pepper flakes

Pinch baking soda

3 pounds ground round

1 large onion, diced

Salt and pepper to taste

One 8-ounce box lasagna noodles

4 eggs, beaten separately and added one at a time (not *separated*)

1 pound mozzarella cheese, shredded

6 ounces (about 1 cup) Parmesan cheese, shredded

---

Prepare a recipe for Basic Tomato Sauce (recipe on page 71). When you are adding the tomatoes to the sauce, add the additional tomato paste, brown sugar, and red pepper flakes. Cook according to directions. When done, stir in the soda (reduces acidity). Set aside.

In the meantime, bring a large pot of water to a boil and cook the lasagna according to package directions until firm but tender, about 8 minutes.

Cook the meat and onions in a large skillet over medium-high heat until the meat is nicely browned and the onions are translucent. Drain excess grease. Set aside.

Preheat the oven to 350°F. Grease a 9 x 13-inch baking dish with olive oil. Assemble the lasagna as follows:

Place a layer of sauce in the bottom of the baking dish. Cover with one layer of pasta strips. Spread a layer of meat over the noodles and pour one beaten egg evenly over the meat. Sprinkle a layer of mozzarella cheese over the meat. Spread tomato sauce lightly on top of the cheese. Repeat layers—noodles, meat, egg (one per layer), cheese, sauce—until all ingredients are used, ending with sauce.

Sprinkle a lush layer of Parmesan cheese over the top, cover with tin foil, and bake for 30 minutes. Remove foil and bake another 10 to 15 minutes until golden brown. Serve with a full-bodied red wine, crusty Italian bread, and spring salad, and you're there. Makes 6 to 8 servings.

## WHAT IS THAT MAN DOING ON THE TABLE?

I know a man whose goal in life is to have a dish that will still be served in a hundred years named after him. He should dig up the PR strategies that put Count Stroganoff, Alfredo di Lello, Figaro, and Jacks on our tables and in our vocabulary.

Beef Stroganoff, a noble slurry of meat, onions, mushrooms, and sour cream, was a favorite of a nineteenth-century Russian diplomat. A Roman restaurateur tossed the first Fettucine Alfredo in the 1920s, boldly naming the dish after himself. If you ever try Figaro Sauce, you'll dine inadvertently with a character in Rossini's *Barber of Seville,* and with every slice of Monterey Jack, you are back in Monterey, California, snacking with a Scottish immigrant named Jacks.

# A Man and His **Clams**

What is it about linguine and clams that brings out the inner-*inamorato* in a man? I know sexy Aphrodite made her Academy Award–winning appearance from the sea-foam on a glorified clam shell, forever intriguing the male imagination, but the way guys get glassy-eyed over this mollusk pasta is remarkable. If the clams aren't laced up with linguine, they have to be steamed; if not steamed, then floating in a chowder.

Like opening the pickle jar, a huge steaming plate of clams makes a man feel dashing, debonair, and desirable. Maybe it's the zinc, maybe it's the garlic, maybe it's the creamy, oozing viscous texture. Ask Tom Cruise; it's likely he will choose his signature garlic-ravaged linguine with zesty red clam sauce as his favorite. This vote is in: To keep him happy as a clam, just cook some. Get hot with Tom's choice or smooth-talk Casanova with the sensuous classic that follows it.

> *When this is good it's very, very good*
> *and when it's limp it's a disaster.*
>
> —Frances Mayes, *Under the Tuscan Sky*

# Tom Cruise's Linguine with Zesty Red Clam Sauce

**Tomato Sauce**

½ cup olive oil

¼ cup cloves garlic, crushed

¼ cup capers, undrained

2 cups chopped parsley,
   plus ½ cup additional for garnish

2 cups chopped plum tomatoes

¾ cup fresh lemon juice

¾ cup dry white wine

½ teaspoon crushed red pepper flakes

1 teaspoon salt

1 heaping teaspoon freshly ground
   black pepper

**Pasta**

1 pound linguine

**Clams**

30 littleneck clams, scrubbed

¼ cup chopped garlic

1 cup dry white wine

1 cup vegetable broth or water

---

To make the tomato sauce: Heat the oil in a large saucepan until hot. Add the garlic and capers, then carefully add the parsley. Stand back because the oil may spatter. Add the tomatoes, lemon juice, wine, peppers flakes, salt, and black pepper. Cook, stirring occasionally, for 15 minutes.

Bring a large pot of salted water to a boil. Add the linguine and cook according to the package directions until firm but tender.

While the pasta is cooking, steam the clams. Place the clams in another large pot with the garlic, wine, and vegetable broth. Cover and bring to a boil over high heat, shaking the pot, until all the shells are open. Leaving the open clams in the pot, drain off all but ¼ cup of the steaming liquid and stir it into the tomato sauce. Cover the clams and keep warm while preparing the rest of the dish.

Drain the linguine and add to the tomato sauce. Cook over high heat for about 4 minutes to heat through.

Divide the pasta among 6 heated bowls. Top each serving with 5 clams and garnish with the remaining parsley. Makes about 4½ cups of sauce and 6 servings.

# Casanova *C*lam Linguine

| | |
|---|---|
| 1 pound linguine | 1 teaspoon white pepper |
| 2 tablespoons olive oil | 1 teaspoon cayenne pepper |
| 8 cloves garlic, very finely chopped | Four 6½-ounce cans chopped clams, |
| ½ cup fresh Italian parsley, chopped | drained; juice reserved |
| ½ cup whipping cream | ¼ pound fresh clams |
| ¼ cup white wine | Freshly grated Parmesan |
| 1 tablespoon Worcestershire sauce | Lemon slices |
| 1 teaspoon garlic salt | |

Prepare the pasta according to package directions.

In heavy skillet, heat the olive oil and sauté the garlic and parsley for 45 seconds over medium-high heat. Reduce heat and add the clam juice, whipping cream, wine, Worcestershire sauce, garlic salt, white and cayenne peppers. Simmer, uncovered, for 10 minutes. Add the chopped clams and fresh clams. Simmer, uncovered, until clams open (5 to 7 minutes).

Serve over the linguine with freshly grated Parmesan and a lemon wedge garnish. Serve with a nice, crisp white wine. Depending on the lusty men who are eating, makes 2 to 4 servings.

*When I think of the food I love*
*it boils down into three categories . . .*
*pasta, pasta, pasta.*

—Peter Beanland

# *You Say Tomato?* I Say **Love A**pple

This succulent, colorful staple has such a fan club that Ella Fitzgerald even sang about it in a flirty little song: "You say 'tomato,' I say 'tom*ah*-to'. . . ." They made it so big in their own movie, *Fried Green Tomatoes,* that according to *Fannie Flagg's Original Whistle Stop Café Cookbook,* "suddenly . . . every café, restaurant, and cafeteria started serving fried green tomatoes." Legend insists that tomatoes actually harbor aphrodisiacal enzymes; maybe that's why they caught on.

The nickname "love apple" is derived from the amorous French phrase *pommes d'amour,* which is the phonetic twin for the misunderstood Italian word for tomato, *pomodoro,* or "fruit of gold." Whichever way you say 'em or fry 'em—fried green tomatoes or fried gold love apples—this creamy adaptation (read, *Yankee*) of a classic Dixieland comfort dish has kept many men I've known singing about *something.*

## **L**ove *A*pple **L**inguine

### From *Goddess in the Kitchen*

| | |
|---|---|
| One 1-pound package linguine or your favorite pasta | 1 teaspoon dill |
| 1 cup unbleached white flour | 1 teaspoon curry powder |
| ¼ cup cornmeal | ½ teaspoon black pepper |
| 2 teaspoons dried basil | ½ teaspoon salt |
| | 1 tablespoon butter |

81

1 tablespoon extra-virgin olive oil

2 cloves garlic, minced

1¼ cups milk

¼ cup wine (white or red, depending
on what you have on hand)

3 big, fat, very firm tomatoes of any
color, cut into ¼-inch slices

Olive oil

Salt and pepper

---

Prepare the pasta, according to package directions, in a large pot of boiling water. While the pasta is cooking, prepare and fry the tomatoes.

In a plastic container with a lid, combine flour, cornmeal, basil, dill, curry powder, pepper, and salt. Cover with the lid and shake, mixing all ingredients well.

Melt butter and oil together in a large skillet over medium-high heat. As the skillet heats up, add the garlic. Place sliced tomatoes in the container, two at a time, and shake gently until tomatoes are completely coated with flour mixture. Plop them in the frying pan.

Fry the love apples for 3 to 4 minutes and flip. Reduce heat to medium and fry for a few minutes more. (If the pan seems dry, pour a little milk or wine in it.) Remove them from skillet and set on a large serving plate. Keep the tomatoes very warm (either on the stove or in a warm oven) but uncovered—we want them crisp!

Reduce heat to medium-low and pour the rest of the milk and wine into the skillet, whisking as you pour. As the sauce begins to heat up, sprinkle about ¼ cup of the remaining flour mixture into the pan, stirring constantly to avoid lumps. If necessary, add more flour mixture to form a nice creamy gravy. Remove sauce from the heat and pour into a gravy boat or decorative bowl.

Drain the pasta, toss it with a little olive oil, and place in 4 pasta dishes. Spoon several fried green love apples on top of the pasta, smother them with the sauce, and serve immediately. Salt and pepper to taste. Makes 4 servings.

# A Rambling Man Has to Eat

Are you living and eating in the fast lane? Take a cooking cue from a working girl. Claiming its origins in the slums of Naples, *pasta putanesca*, or more graphically, "whore's pasta," is so quick to toss together that ladies of the hour can whip up this robust meal of olives, garlic, tomatoes, capers, and anchovies between clients for a little extra zest to do good work.

If you are a man of today's world moving at a quasar's pace, maybe your gypsy soul needs a little nourishment, *alla zingara*, in the spirit of a bohemian babe. Traditionally, this garnish of chopped ham, tongue, mushrooms, truffles, and Madeira-laced tomato sauce with meat, poultry, or eggs was served by gypsy women to their roving men.

You say you're short on time, tongue, truffles, and gypsy girls but still feeling like a famished rogue? Take ten and let the universe spin on its own while you go toss a pie that will liberate the laid-back *bon vivant* in you and satisfy your wild side.

*'Tis an ill cook that cannot lick his own fingers.*

—Shakespeare

# Pizza Alla Zingara

**No-Rise Pizza Dough**
From *Wild Women in the Kitchen*
1 cup unbleached white flour
⅓ cup hot water
2 tablespoons olive oil
Pinch of salt

**The Topping**
8 ounces mushrooms, sliced
2 tablespoons Madeira wine

3 cups Basic Tomato Sauce
(see page 71)
¾ pound deli ham, cut into small
cubes
2 garlic cloves, finely chopped
2 cups (about ½ pound) mozzarella
cheese, shredded
1 tablespoon crushed red pepper
flakes

---

Mix the dough ingredients together in a large bowl and knead for 5 minutes. Let rest 5 minutes before rolling out.

Preheat oven to 425°F. Dust a clean work surface lightly with flour, place the dough on surface, spread it out and flatten with fingers or rolling pin to a ¼-inch thickness, forming a large rectangle (about 12 x 15 inches). Dust a large sheet or pizza pan with flour and place dough on the pan, stretching it to reach all sides.

In a large saucepan, sauté the mushrooms in the Madeira wine over medium heat for 2 to 3 minutes. Remove from heat. Using a kitchen spoon, smooth a thin layer of Basic Tomato Sauce over pizza dough all the way to the edges.

Sprinkle with ham, garlic, and sautéed mushrooms and blanket everything with mozzarella. Sprinkle with red pepper flakes and bake for 20 minutes, or until golden brown on bottom and cheese is melted. Serve immediately. Makes 2 to 3 servings.

# **B**ohemian B.L.T. *Pizza*

**The Dough**

1 Pillsbury™ Pizza Crust in a can,
  or any no-rise pizza dough recipe

**The Pizza**

1 tablespoon cornmeal

¾ pound bacon, cooked, blotted,
  and crumbled

2½ cups mozzarella cheese, shredded

4 to 5 plum tomatoes, diced

2 tablespoons mayonnaise

Salt and pepper

2 cups lettuce, shredded

---

Preheat the oven to 425°F. Make pizza dough according to the directions, lightly grease a pizza pan with olive oil or spray oil, and dust with cornmeal. Roll out dough, line the pan, and cook for 6 minutes. Cool.

When the crust is cooled, spread cooked and crumbled bacon over the crust and top with mozzarella cheese. Return pizza to oven and bake for an additional 8 to 10 minutes until bubbling. Remove from oven and cool. Mix diced tomatoes with mayonnaise, salt, and pepper. Drain any juice. Sprinkle this mixture over pizza and top with shredded lettuce. Serves 2 to 3.

*A nickel will get you on the subway,*
*but garlic will get you a seat.*

—Old New York proverb

## *Feeling Fine* with Some Good Ol' **R&R**

When a jeweler at Molina in Scottsdale, Arizona, hinted that he would trade me a Cartier™ pen for an authentic plate of Spanish rice and beans, tell me no more. . . . I was off on a quest. I soon discovered there is literally a world of difference between Spanish rice and *beans* (R&B) and their "separated at birth" twin, the classic southern soul dish, red beans and rice (R&R). Regardless of different techniques and taste, however, both are renowned for the way they swagger in a man's mind.

In the delicious cookbook, *Jazz Cooks,* bassist Richard Davis and crooner Harry Connick Jr. count the Crescent City staple red beans and rice as cool favorites and share their recipes. Jazz giant Louis Armstrong was known to spice up personal letters with his trademark sign-off, "Red beans and ricely yours, Louis," and in *LaBelle Cuisine,* the high priestess of good vibrations, Patti LaBelle, swears her R&R are "bound to light your fire." Paul Newman says he "would kill for" a variation of ham hocks and lima beans, but that's a different pot.

After all the excitement, my search brought me to my own mailbox. My Spanish-blooded friend Linda Graber sent her mom's "get down" recipe for Spanish R&B, and one of my best men, Indiana University track coach Wayne Pate, who has "New Orleans" written all over his birth certificate, shared this R&R recipe. So I'm off to pick out my Cartier pen and scribble "de-lish" all over this fiery dish.

# Coach Pate's *Cajun* R&R

1 pound (about 2 cups) dried red beans
1 beef bouillon cube
¾ teaspoon kosher salt
6 to 7 cups water, divided
1½ cups uncooked long-grain white
  rice (not brown!)
1 pound smoked sausage
1 cup ham, cubed
½ large onion, chopped

3 large mushrooms, sliced
½ cup medium salsa (prefers
  Newman's Own)
2 tablespoons Big Easy Creole
  Seasoning (recipe follows)
¾ teaspoon dried thyme leaves
½ teaspoon ground sage
Salt and pepper
Tabasco

## Big Easy Creole Seasoning

¼ cup kosher salt
1 tablespoon powdered garlic
1 tablespoon cracked black pepper
1 tablespoon paprika

¾ teaspoon onion powder
½ teaspoon cayenne pepper
½ teaspoon dried thyme
½ teaspoon dried oregano leaves

---

To make the Creole seasoning, simply mix all listed ingredients together. Store in a glass jar in a cool, dark place and use as needed. Easy as that!

Prepare the beans one of two ways: After rinsing them and sorting through them to remove debris and defective beans, soak the beans overnight (or at least 5 hours) in enough water to cover by 3 inches. Or, place the rinsed beans in a pot or Dutch oven, cover with 3 inches of cold water, and bring to boil over high heat. Boil for 3 minutes. Remove the beans from the heat and let stand, covered, for 1 hour. In each case, drain and rinse before using.

Place the beans and bouillon cube in a Dutch oven or large pot and add just enough fresh, cold water to cover them (about 4 cups). Cover and bring to a boil over high heat. Reduce the heat to medium-low and simmer, covered, for 45 minutes.

Add 2 more cups of water, rice, smoked sausage, ham, onion, mushrooms, salsa, Big Easy Creole Seasoning, dried thyme, and sage. Increase heat and bring to a boil.

Reduce heat to medium-low and simmer the R&R, pot lid slightly askew (to release a little steam), for 1½ to 2 hours. Stir occasionally and cook until the rice is tender, adding more water if necessary.

In the last 10 to 15 minutes of cooking, season with salt, pepper, and as much Tabasco or favorite hot red pepper sauce as you can bear. Serve with baguettes in large bowls. Makes 6 generous servings.

### THE INSIDE LINE

The truth is, Coach Pate simply uses a large crock pot. First, he mixes the beans, beef bouillon, salt, sausage, ham, onions, and mushrooms in the crock pot and adds enough water to cover all the ingredients. He cranks his crock pot to HIGH and cooks everything for an hour.

Then Coach Pate adds the salsa, McCormick™ Creole Seasoning, thyme, sage, and Tabasco. He cooks this for 4 hours, adding water as needed. Finally, he adds the rice, cooks the batch for one more hour, and serves. Kitchen R&R—easy as that.

## Our Brothers of Perpetual Indulgence

Mycophiles unite! These little phallic-formed fungi certainly have a fan club of priapic proportions. Freud was a mushroom lover; I wonder if he disclosed his fungal fixation to his therapist? And what of the truffle obsession of ages? "Whosoever says, *truffle,* utters a grand word, which awakens erotic and gastronomic ideas. . . ," proclaimed über-epicure Brillat-Savarin. Truffles have been prized for centuries and were credited by the ancient Greeks and Romans with both therapeutic and aphrodisiac powers.

Not everyone is a mushroom man, however. English botanist John Gerard wrote of the mushroom in 1597: "It has a mischievous quality. . . . Few of them are good to be eaten and most of them do suffocate and strangle the eater."

Authors Benjamin Lewis and Rodrigo Velloso rebut with, "*Eat Dangerously*!" They tip the scales for good by adding, "Moliére said that you are responsible for what you don't do as well as for what you do. This means that if you don't eat great food because someone tells you it's unhealthy, that's nobody's fault but your own. . . . Bring it on!"

> *All the things I really like to do are*
> *either illegal, immoral, or fattening.*
>
> —Alexander Woollcot

# Risotto ai Funghi Porcini *(Porcini Mushroom Risotto)*

From the *Eat Dangerously Cookbook*

1½ cup porcini mushrooms, dried
1 cup hot water
2 cups chicken or beef stock
1 tablespoon butter
¼ cup extra-virgin olive oil
½ shallot, minced
1½ cups Italian Arborio rice
1 cup Chivas Imperial™, Johnnie Walker™ Blue Label, or other eighteen-year-old blended Scotch

½ cup Parmigiano Reggiano cheese, freshly grated
1 tablespoon fresh parsley, chopped
Cheese and parsley garnish
Salt and freshly ground pepper

Soak the mushrooms in 1 cup hot water for 10 to 15 minutes. Remove the mushrooms and squeeze out the liquid. Dice the mushrooms and set aside.

Strain the remaining liquid into saucepan, add stock, and simmer on a back burner while you continue with your creation. Add salt and pepper to taste.

In a larger heavy-bottomed pan, melt the butter and olive oil over medium heat. Add the shallot and sauté for 1 minute; add the mushrooms and rice and stir for a few more minutes.

Pour the whisky over the rice and carefully ignite. Allow flame to rage for about 30 seconds, cover briefly to extinguish, and then remove the cover, allowing the remaining spirits to evaporate.

Add one ladle of the stock mixture to the rice and stir until the liquid has almost completely evaporated. Repeat this process, keeping the risotto cooking at a slow boil until you have added all the beef stock mixture (if the rice seems a bit hard, feel free to add a little more water). Cook the rice until it is *al dente* and all the liquid has evaporated, about 15 minutes (note your time for the future).

Remove the risotto from the heat and gently stir in the grated Parmigiano Reggiano cheese and chopped parsley. Allow the risotto to rest, covered, for a few minutes, and then serve immediately. Garnish with additional Parmigiano Reggiano cheese and parsley; season with salt and pepper to taste. Makes 4 dangerously delicious servings.

*The truffles themselves have been interrogated, and have answered simply: Eat us and praise the Lord.*

—Alexandre Dumas

# Fowl Play

## A Thing for Wings . . . and Breasts and Legs and Thighs

He eats nothing but doves, love;
and that breeds hot blood,
and hot blood begets hot thoughts, and hot
  thoughts beget hot deeds,
and hot deeds is love.
—Shakespeare, *Troilus and Cressida*

HE LOVES . . .

**S**eared turkey drumsticks; I fantasize about them for several days after.—*Tom, Delaware*

**D**orismarie's fried chicken . . . what else?!!—*Peter, Colorado*

**A** chicken quesadilla and seltzer water with lime.—*Michael, New York*

**B**roiled chicken wings with a zesty peanut dipping sauce. . . .—*Peter, California*

**R**oast turkey with gravy, chestnut and sausage stuffing, cranberry-orange sauce, mashed turnips . . . and pumpkin chiffon pie.—*Richard, Nevada*

**C**hicken and dumplings. . . .—*Bob, a Hungarian from Pennsylvania*

# Her Scepter Is Her **Frying Pan**

Every man I know who has tasted Dorismarie Welcher's fried chicken wings has flipped out over them. When I first met the self-styled "Queen of the Hudson" more than twenty years ago, she was living in Aspen, Colorado, managing a household of twentysomething young bachelors whose only purpose in life was to party and ski. She'd cook up batch after fabulous batch of her famous chicken wings and used them as bribes, along with plates of her Cowboy Cookies, to get these guys to clean up their act, wash the windows, pick up the house, and take out the garbage. The windows gleamed.

Our friendship has endured for a quarter of a century. I keep my crystal cookie jar filled with *the* famous Cowboy Cookies (for more cookie lore, turn to page 182), and Dorismarie still whips up her wings for the lucky souls who visit her as she rules the Hudson River from her "Fantasy Island" New York City apartment. Magic happens when the Queen herself is ruling the skillet, but with her recipe in hand, you now hold the key to a quintessential feel-good favorite.

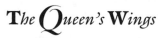

### The Queen's Wings

From *Goddess in the Kitchen*

| | |
|---|---|
| 2 pounds plump chicken wings | 2 teaspoons black pepper, coarsely |
| Juice of one lemon | ground |

| | |
|---|---|
| 1½ teaspoons kosher salt | ¾ cup flour |
| Paprika | ½ teaspoon ground turmeric (optional) |
| Ground cayenne pepper | Canola or peanut oil for frying |

---

Prepare the wings by removing the tips (they burn too quickly), cutting them in half at the joint. Sprinkle the lemon juice over the wings and blanket with salt and black pepper. Sprinkle the wings with paprika and a dash of cayenne pepper to taste and let rest for 5 minutes.

Combine the flour, turmeric if using, and a few more dashes of cayenne in a brown paper or plastic bag and shake it up (you can always use a little Lawry's™ seasoned salt).

Cover the bottom of a heavy black iron skillet with a generous amount of oil and heat to very hot but not smoking (a drop of water should bounce off it) over medium-high heat. Shake the wing pieces, 2 or 3 at a time, in the bag of flour. Shake off excess flour and fry the wings for 2 to 3 minutes, skin side down, until they are golden.

Reduce the heat just a touch, turn the wings over with tongs, and cook for about 5 more minutes, turning them a few times to get them nice and crispy. Season with more salt, pepper, and paprika to taste.

Transfer the wings to a brown paper bag or paper towels on the counter so they can drain. Arrange on a platter in an attractive "fan" and serve with Cadillac Ranch Dip (recipe follows) or alone. Makes 2 to 4 servings of The Queen's Wings, depending on how many guys are at the table.

---

# Cadillac Ranch Dip

½ cup buttermilk
½ cup sour cream
½ cup white wine vinegar
¼ cup extra-virgin olive oil
1 tablespoon Dijon mustard
2 teaspoons Worcestershire
  sauce
2 teaspoons honey

1½ teaspoons lemon juice, freshly
  squeezed
1½ teaspoons tarragon leaves
1 teaspoon basil leaves
¾ teaspoon oregano leaves
¾ teaspoon salt
½ teaspoon garlic powder
¼ teaspoon black pepper

Measure all ingredients (all spices are dried) into a blender and torch to emulsify! Refrigerate for at least 8 hours. Shake (or blend gently) before serving and pour into a decorative bowl.

*I count myself in nothing else so happy*
*As in a soul remembering my good friends.*

—Shakespeare

# Just Call It "**P**ure **C**ure"

If chicken soup is "Jewish penicillin," then the cockle-warming Chicken Dumplings Divine is a Pennsylvania Dutch triple bypass surgery connecting the heart to the soul via the stomach. In the old German communities of Pennsylvania (they aren't Dutch at all), this favorite meal is called "potpie" and is not to be confused with shepherd's pie or the frozen food-type "pot pie." This is the chicken 'n' dumplings of which men's dreams are made.

When my first book, *Goddess in the Kitchen,* came out I was invited to the TV Food Network show *In Food Today* to do a segment on "Sacred Foods" with host and author David Rosengarten. I thought, "Perfect. I can demonstrate a once-sacred recipe like hot cross buns with their pagan roots honoring the fertility goddess Eastre." How wrong I was; they had their hearts set on my version of Chicken Stew for the Soul and wanted me to illumine the sacred tradition of sharing meals together as a family, blessing the food, eating with joy.

The show's crowning moment came after we were off the air and finished our "beauty shot" ("Smile and stir . . . smile and stir . . ."). The host, with chicken "potpie" trickling down his chin, was slurping up every drop in his bowl, and the camera crew was standing in line—spoons in hand—eagerly waiting to pay homage to the sacred stew. Not one drop remained.

# *C*hicken **D**umplings **D**ivine

**The Stew**

One 4-pound chicken or 4 chicken
  breasts, skinned
2½ to 3 quarts water
2 chicken bouillon cubes
½ onion, chopped

**The Divine Dumplings**

4 cups unbleached white flour
1 teaspoon salt
Dash of mace
1 tablespoon cold butter
2 eggs
1 cup milk

---

In a large pot, cover the chicken with water and bring to a full boil over medium-high heat. Reduce heat, add the chicken bouillon and onion, and continue cooking the chicken at a low boil until chicken is done but not quite "fallin' off the bones," approximately 30 minutes. Turn off the heat; remove the chicken from the broth and remove the bones. Chop the chicken meat coarsely and return it to the broth—heat still off.

While the stew is brewing, make the dumplings. Mix the flour, salt, and mace in a large bowl. Cut the butter into the flour with a fork; add eggs and milk and mix until the dough is smooth. Divide the dough into four portions and knead each piece of dough slightly; cover with a towel and set aside.

Put the broth back on the heat and bring it to a rolling boil. On a well-floured surface, roll the dough to a ¼-inch thickness and cut into 2- to 3-inch-square "dumplings." Drop them one by one into the boiling broth (Mom's advice: "Follow the 'bubbles'").

Stir occasionally to keep the dough from sticking together as it boils. After all the dough has been dropped in the pot, turn the heat down to low and simmer stew with the lid on for about 20 minutes, until it thickens a bit. Smile and stir the stew for a few more minutes, until it is irresistibly creamy. Makes 6 servings.

> *After a good dinner one can forgive anybody,*
> *even one's own relations.*
>
> —Oscar Wilde,
> *A Woman of No Importance*

## Like a Rooster *in the* **Hen House**

It's time to let all men in on a secret: Every wise woman I know has one specific signature "seduction dish" in her recipe file that she uses to lure a man into her universe (C'mon guys, I didn't say web . . . ). If she's really wise, she subtly finds out a man's favorite food and prepares it accordingly (not, "Baits the hook accordingly . . ."). She stirs up his appetite and satiates the senses with a damn good dish.

When I discovered a fantastic recipe for Tipper Gore's Spiced Roast Chicken in one of my cherished cookbooks, *Comfort Foods from Mothers' Voices,* I had to wonder if it was Tipper's chicken that did it for First Man Al . . . or was it her Tennessee Treats (to order the cookbook, please see page 219). Bob Hope loved his chicken hash, and I know that Kevin Costner sees stars when served good Mexican food accompanied by chilled pineapple juice, no ice.

My friend Kristina—hubby Carl will attest—swears by her "man-catcher" Chicken Ruby ("If you want to reel him in from the sea and get him in the boat"). Another culinary courtesan wrote, "Each man in my life can be identified by the dish I won his heart with." And then L. J., the mysterious kitchen temptress, stepped forth with her secret recipe, saying, "Here's something I always relied on the first time I had a man over to dinner, because it's good and easy and I know it works (and who needs anxieties on such an occasion?)." L. J.'s mom inherited the recipe from *her* mother . . . and L. J. is happily married. And Kevin, if you're reading, my single friends are just waiting to make you chicken enchiladas and chill your juice.

# L. J.'s Jewish Chinese Chicken

One 3½- to 4-pound chicken or
  4 large breasts
1 cup honey
¾ cup soy sauce

¾ cup sherry
½-inch fresh ginger root, peeled
  and minced
2 garlic cloves, finely minced

---

Preheat the oven to 450°F. Rinse the chicken, removing the neck and giblets, and place it on a rack inside a roasting pan, breast side up. Combine the honey, soy sauce, sherry, ginger, and garlic. Brush the entire chicken with honey mixture, put it in the oven, and immediately reduce heat to 350°F.

Use the remaining mixture to baste the bird at 10- to 15-minute intervals as it roasts for approximately an hour (20 minutes per pound; less for breasts). When it has a nice dark glaze, it's done. Complete the meal with rice and Sweet Baby Carrots (men go crazy over them; recipe follows) and use the liquid from the pan to pour over the rice. Makes 4 servings (or 2 servings with leftovers). *L'chayim!*

# Sweet Baby Carrots

½ cup (1 stick) butter
½ cup white sugar
½ cup brown sugar

1 pound baby carrots
2 cups water
Nutmeg

---

In a medium saucepan, melt the butter over medium-low heat and add the white and brown sugars, stirring until they dissolve. Add the carrots and pour enough water over them to *just cover* them.

Cook the carrots, covered, until they are almost tender; remove them from the pan. Continue cooking the liquid for 5 to 7 minutes, until it reduces to a nice glaze. Add a tiny pinch of nutmeg. Return the baby carrots to the glaze and cook together for 2 to 3 minutes more. Serve immediately. Makes 4 servings.

*At a dinner-party one should eat wisely
but not too well, and talk well but not too wisely.*

—W. Somerset Maugham

# Chicken Artichoke Enchiladas

One 3½-pound chicken, skinned, quartered, cooked, and shredded

Three 14½-ounce cans low-sodium chicken broth

4 tablespoons extra-virgin olive oil, divided

1 large onion, finely chopped

One 13¾-ounce can artichoke hearts in water, drained and chopped

4 to 5 cloves garlic, chopped

½ teaspoon dried oregano

½ teaspoon ground cumin

¼ teaspoon ground cinnamon

3 tablespoons chili powder

| | |
|---|---|
| 1 tablespoon flour | ½ pound Monterey Jack cheese, |
| Salt and pepper | coarsely grated (about 2 cups) |
| Eight 5- to 6-inch flour tortillas | ½ cup black olives, sliced |

---

Place the chicken in the broth in a heavy-bottomed pot and bring to a boil over medium heat. Reduce heat to medium-low and simmer the chicken, pot lid askew, until chicken is cooked, about 30 minutes. Remove the chicken to a large cutting board; when it has cooled, debone it and coarsely shred or chop the meat. Strain and reserve the broth.

Heat 2 tablespoons of olive oil in large saucepan over medium-low heat. Add approximately ½ cup chopped onion (reserve the rest), chopped artichoke hearts, garlic, oregano, cumin, and cinnamon. Cover and cook for 10 minutes, stirring occasionally, until the onion is tender.

Mix in the chili powder and flour and stir for several minutes. Gradually whisk in 2 to 2½ cups of the chicken broth. Increase the heat a bit and bring the sauce to a low boil, stirring occasionally, until it has reduced to a nice creamy consistency (about 25 minutes). Remove from heat and season with salt and pepper.

Heat approximately 1 teaspoon of oil in a medium skillet over medium heat. Cook one tortilla at a time until soft, about 20 seconds per side. Transfer to a surface lined with paper towels. Repeat with remaining tortillas, adding oil as needed.

Spread ½ cup of enchilada sauce on the bottom of a 9 x 13-inch glass baking dish. Mix one-half of the remaining sauce with the chicken. Reserve the other half for a topping.

Arrange the tortillas on a work surface. Ladle ¼ cup of the chicken-artichoke mixture down the center of each tortilla; then sprinkle 2 to 3 tablespoons of cheese,

1 tablespoon of olives, and 1 tablespoon of onion over the top of the chicken. Roll up tortillas and lay seam side down in the prepared dish.

Preheat oven to 375°F. Top the enchiladas with the remaining sauce and sprinkle with any remaining cheese (grate more if necessary). Cover the dish with foil and bake for 20 minutes; remove the foil and bake for another 10 minutes, until sauce starts to bubble. Let stand for 5 to 10 minutes before serving. Makes 4 servings.

### THE INSIDE LINE

In case you have hot plans and want to minimize kitchen time, assemble the enchiladas in advance. Just cover and refrigerate them without the sauce on top; add the sauce when you bake them. If they are chilled when going in the oven, cook with the foil on for 10 minutes longer (30 minutes total).

*The sight of her face . . . together with the maddening fragrance of food, evoked an emotion of a wild tenderness and hunger in him which was unutterable.*

—Thomas Wolfe, *April, Late April*

# You Know These Breasts Will **Not Fade Away**

Writers spend a lot of time in "the zone," a creative safe haven where conversations from grocery store lines get woven into tomorrow's hard copy; where fragments of dreams pour out onto a page in the coffee-laced daze of the morning's deadline. Ben Fong-Torres, former wordsmith at *Rolling Stone* magazine and author of four books, including *Not Fade Away: A Backstage Pass to 20 Years of Rock and Roll* and *The Rice Room: Growing Up Chinese-American,* has done some time in the zone. Let's visit and talk food. . . .

Having been born into a Chinese restaurant family, I naturally detested the idea of cooking as I grew up. In my twenties, working at *Rolling Stone,* I made do with canned food, scrambled eggs with Spam™, and other people's restaurants. It took Connie McCole, who taught a "Timesavers" cooking course out of her oversized kitchen in San Francisco, to turn me into a cook. Looking like Mitzi Gaynor in an apron, she'd whip through a full-course dinner in front of twelve students, using fresh ingredients and finishing—and serving—everything in under an hour.

I was hooked, and soon began turning out *Bul Kogi, Poisson en Papillote, Charcuterie,* and my favorite, Chicken Breasts with Pecans. I learned to make appetizers, various rice and pasta dishes, soups, salads, vegetables, and desserts, from almond *gateau* to *zabaglione.*

But you know what? I still like Spam.

# Ben's Fantasy Pecan-Covered Breasts

6 ounces pecans (about 1½ cups),
  ground
10 tablespoons butter, divided
2 tablespoons Dijon mustard
4 chicken breasts, skinned and boned
2 tablespoons corn oil

**Sauce**
⅓ cup sour cream
1 teaspoon Dijon mustard
Salt and pepper

---

Sprinkle the ground pecans on a sheet of wax paper. Melt 6 tablespoons of butter in a small saucepan. Remove from heat and whisk in 2 tablespoons of mustard (it will look curdled but will smooth out). Dip each chicken breast into this mixture and then coat with pecans, patting them onto the chicken.

Melt the remaining 4 tablespoons of butter with the corn oil in a large sauté pan over medium heat. Sauté the chicken for 3 to 4 minutes per side, until it "springs" back when touched. Remove from the pan and keep in a low oven.

To make the sauce, return the pan to medium-low heat and deglaze it with sour cream, scraping up all the leftover pecans with a spatula. (*Note:* Don't let the sauce boil or it will curdle.) Add the mustard and season with salt and pepper to taste. To serve, spoon some sauce on each plate and place a chicken breast on top. Makes 4 servings.

# A Chicken *in a* Pan by Any Other Name

If you travel across the Mediterranean to the shores of the Dead Sea and the Hashemite Kingdom of Jordan, *paella*—a Spanish dish of spiced rice, meats, shellfish, and veggies (sometimes even snails) made in a two-handled shallow *paella* (pan)—becomes *maglooba*.

Mag-LOO-ba . . . same pan, chicken or lamb, rice with exotic spices, aubergines . . . no pork, ever. Jeff Ogren, a homesick Peace Corps volunteer, gave me the inside line:

> Being in the middle of nowhere makes food all the more enjoyable. The nearest butcher is nearly an entire day's journey away. The chicken is butchered in front of you, while you wait; it doesn't get any fresher. Camel, well, I have yet to get up the nerve to try it. I spend most nights fantasizing about what I will eat when I return to the U.S. . . . juicy steaks cooked on the grill, Mom's beef stroganoff, Grandma's tomato soup, pork chops (impossible to find in an Islamic country), and apple sauce!
>
> So I have developed a taste for local foods. With maglooba, which literally means "upside down," you dump the pot of chicken (or lamb) on a serving platter and everyone eats off of that platter—kind of a group exercise. Well, Dad, fire up the grill; I'll be home soon. Oh, and Sis, did you make that blueberry pie?

Maglooba is served. . . . We're not in Kansas anymore.

# ℳ*aglooba*

| | |
|---|---|
| 2 aubergines (about 3½ pounds), peeled and sliced | 1 tablespoon salt |
| Water and salt to soak the aubergines | 1 teaspoon allspice |
| ½ cup extra-virgin olive oil | ¾ teaspoon cinnamon |
| One 3½- to 4-pound chicken, cut into pieces | ¼ teaspoon cardamom |
| 4 cups water | 1½ cups long grain white rice |
| | ¼ cup clarified butter |
| | ½ cup pine nuts |

Soak the aubergines in lightly salted water for 20 minutes; remove and pat the pieces dry. Fry them in olive oil in a large sauté pan over medium-high heat for 4 to 5 minutes, until they are browned.

Place the chicken in a wide-mouthed stock pot or paella pan, cover with 4 cups of water and 1 tablespoon of salt and bring to a boil. Reduce heat to medium-low and skim the top of the pot, removing pieces of excess fats and skin. Add the allspice, cinnamon, and cardamom and simmer, covered, for 40 to 45 minutes, until meat is tender.

Remove the chicken from the pot; strain and reserve the stock into another container. Return ¼ cup of chicken stock mixed with 2 to 3 tablespoons of rice to the pot and sauté, stirring over medium heat for a few minutes.

Add the chicken and the aubergines, stir well, and then add the remaining measure of rice. Gradually ladle the entire amount of chicken stock back into the pan. Cook, uncovered, at a low boil over low heat for 30 minutes or until rice is firm but tender and the stock has been absorbed (add more water—or even a splash of wine—if necessary to avoid dryness).

In a sauté pan, fry the pine nuts in the butter (to clarify butter, see page 61) until golden and toasted. Serve maglooba by inverting the paella pan upside down onto a serving platter. Scatter the pine nuts on top of the dish and dig in. Makes 4 servings.

*A man's palate can, in time,*
*become accustomed to anything.*

—Napoleon Bonaparte

---

## This **Bird Rules** Men's Roost

When it comes to food men love, does a traditional Thanksgiving turkey dinner even need an introduction? Let the gents tell you themselves: "My favorite meal? Turkey and dressing with all the trimmings. The dressing has to be made from our yellow cornmeal according to my mom's tried-and-true recipe; the turkey is best if it's free-range. Fix it with sweet potatoes, carrot casserole, green beans, and our traditional Jell-O™ apple-pineapple salad . . . and, if we can sit upright, apple or mincemeat pie."

And again: "Roast turkey with gravy, chestnut and sausage stuffing, cranberry-orange sauce, mashed turnips, four-onion creamed onions, and pumpkin chiffon pie." Well I'm proud to say, "I have you covered." Give thanks and enjoy.

*The pleasures of the table are for every man,*
*of every land and no matter of what place*
*in history or society;*
*they can be part of all his other pleasures,*
*and they last the longest, to console him*
*when he has outlived the rest.*

—Brillat-Savarin

# Baptized Bird with Harvest Butter Rum Stuffing

**Bird Bath**

One 12- to 14-pound young turkey,
   thawed
2 gallons iced water
2 to 3 cups milk
1 cup kosher salt

**Bird Baste**

Olive oil
Salt and pepper
1 teaspoon sage
¼ cup butter, melted
2 tablespoons rum
1 cup chicken stock (canned will do)

**Harvest Butter Rum Stuffing**

½ cup dried cherries
⅓ cup rum
7 cups dried French bread, sliced into
   1-inch cubes
2 cups cornbread, cubed
2 medium Golden Delicious apples,
   peeled and cut into ½-inch cubes
1 large stalk celery, diced
1 small onion, chopped
1 tablespoon dried sage
1 teaspoon kosher salt
½ teaspoon black pepper
2 eggs, beaten
4 tablespoons butter, melted
½ cup hot water

---

Remove the neck and giblets from the turkey (you can use them to make giblet broth for gravy). Place the bird, breasts down if possible, in a clean 5-gallon bucket or even in a clean sink. Rub with salt and let rest for 15 minutes. Next, baptize the turkey with milk and water and let it soak for 1 to 2 hours (the longer the better), turning it over once during this time.

Soak the cherries in the rum while you prepare the stuffing. In a large bowl, mix the French bread and cornbread cubes, apples, celery, onion, sage, salt, and pepper. Pour the eggs and butter over the stuffing and then gently fold in the cherries. Finally, pour hot water over everything and stir until it is moist and sticky.

Preheat the oven to 450°F. Remove the bird from its bathwater and let it drain completely. Loosely stuff the bird, truss it properly by binding the legs together with a string or wire (secures the stuffing inside the bird), and nestle it a large roasting pan.

Anoint the entire bird with extra-virgin olive oil and sprinkle with salt, pepper, and dried sage. Roast on lowest level of the oven for 30 minutes.

Blend the chicken stock, butter, and rum together. Remove the bird from the oven, baste it thoroughly with the butter-rum mixture, and cover with aluminum foil. Insert a probe thermometer into thickest part of the thigh and return it to the oven, reducing temperature to 325°F. Continue basting the bird every 20 minutes or so while it roasts. When the thermometer reads 175°F it should be done (a stuffed turkey this size could require a total of to 3½ to 4 hours of roasting). Let the bird rest, loosely covered, for 15 minutes before carving. (You can make a turkey giblet gravy or the Great Crater Gravy on page 155).

Transfer the stuffing into a decorative bowl. Serve with all the trimmings of your dreams and give thanks to the cook! Makes 8 to 10 servings.

# His Dish

## Favorite Feasts from Wild Waters

Divine Aphrodite,
much celebrated lover of laughter . . .
Companion of Bacchus, whose bliss is abundant,
Patroness of the feasts which last for nights . . .

—Homer, *The Iliad*

# Is Fish

HE LOVES . . .

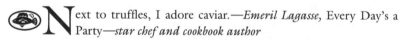 **N**ext to truffles, I adore caviar.—*Emeril Lagasse,* Every Day's a Party—*star chef and cookbook author*

**G**rilled calamari from the Croatian coast.—*Vojko, Slovenia*

**F**resh Pike Quenelle with a spiny lobster sauce. . . .—*Chef Jean-Pierre Doignon, France and Nevada*

**C**eviche; an Ecuadorian dish prepared of seafood marinated in fruit juice.—*Patricio, Ecuador*

**L**obster tail and shrimp . . . always a favorite.—*A New York gentleman*

**S**ushi, sushi, sushi.—*Zack, Tennessee*

## Let's Go **Spanish Fly** Fishing

Cancel your prescription for Spanish fly—that notorious beetle-dust love potion revered for its power to "transform a man, even an old man, into a wonderfully functioning sexual machine that is capable of satisfying his partner for six hours, without a pause—without exception." (Be forewarned; the stuff can also kill you.) And before you gobble too much Viagra®, heed the—shall we say, deflating—truth of Dr. Ruth: "The greatest lover in the world cannot give a woman an orgasm unless she *allows* herself to have it. But men dream on."

Bacchants and gentlemen, toss your performance pressures in the river and just go fishing. Seafood is *the* food, the tried-and-true aphrodisiacs from the home surf of the Goddess of Love, Aphrodite. You've heard it before: "Eat your oysters." Of course, the most dashing way to consume these "queens of aphrodisiac cuisine" is on their pearly half-shells, *au naturel,* spritzed with fresh lemon and cocktail and Tabasco sauce *en garde;* no recipe necessary. But you also might be seduced by "angels and devils on horseback" (oysters wrapped or covered with bacon and broiled), get high on Oysters Bienville, a Crescent City gem, and boost your ego with the Orgiastic Oysters, found in the frisky cookbook *Wild Women in the Kitchen.*

Meanwhile, kick back, relax, and bait your ardent appetite with a simple, tactical aphrodisiac: the charismatic crab cake.

# Classic *C*rab Cakes

| | |
|---|---|
| 1 pound crab meat (Blue crab is best) | Pepper to taste |
| 2 eggs | Dash of Tabasco or favorite hot pepper |
| 2 tablespoons mayonnaise | sauce |
| 1 tablespoon horseradish | ½ to ¾ cup Saltine™-type cracker |
| 1½ teaspoons Old Bay™ Seasoning | crumbs |
| 1 tablespoon fresh parsley, finely | Flour to dust cakes |
| chopped | 2 tablespoons extra-virgin olive oil |
| ¼ teaspoon salt | 1 tablespoon butter |

Combine all ingredients in a large bowl except crackers and flour. By hand, form 8 crab cakes; do not pack too tightly. Roll crackers into fine crumbs, roll each cake in the crumbs, and pat the crumbs lightly into the cake. Lightly flour the cakes. Cover and refrigerate for at least 1 hour.

Heat the olive oil and butter in a large skillet over medium-high heat. Fry the cakes until golden brown, 3 to 4 minutes per side, turning once. Drain on paper towels. Serves 2 to 4 bacchants.

*I will not eat oysters. I want my food dead—*
*not sick, not wounded—dead.*

—Woody Allen

# Kill the Cat with This **H**angover Helper

Blame it on the oyster shooters: Your lust for life penetrated such new heights and stratospheres that you were table-dancing at the bar while the women swooned and the men turned an envious eye . . . and you polished off a fifth of Herradura.

The Germans describe it best—*Katzenjammer*—miserable cat's whining. The freight train roars between your ears, your body feels like the marrow has been sucked out of it. *Katzenjammer.* You could brave a prairie oyster—not to be confused with Rocky Mountain oysters—a hangover remedy of one whole raw egg, one-half teaspoon of vinegar, pepper, and salt in a shot glass. Agostera bitters in seltzer might take off the edge. But baby, I say you need *the cure.*

Traditionally *the cure* is served after a night out partying, sometime midday, fortified with ice-cold beer, good bread, *canguil, tostado,* and plantain chips. This authentic recipe was dictated over the phone to my brother the day after his thirtysomething birthday party by his friend in Ecuador.

Patricio adds, "I know it seems weird to use ketchup, but when it was introduced to South America in the '20s and '30s, ketchup was considered quite a delicacy and was used to create many dishes. It really is the key ingredient."

*Food comes first, then morals.*

—Bertolt Brecht, *The Threepenny Opera*

# Ceviche Ecuatoriano

Juice of 12 large limes
¼ teaspoon sugar
2 large Bermuda onions, thinly sliced and quartered
1¼ cups premium or freshly squeezed orange juice
1¼ cups ketchup
2 tablespoons olive oil
1 to 2 teaspoons Tabasco
1 yellow bell pepper, seeded and diced
1 red bell pepper, seeded and diced
1 large ripe tomato, seeded and chopped
3 tablespoons cilantro, finely chopped
3 tablespoons Italian parsley, finely chopped
1 pound fresh mushrooms, scrubbed and quartered (optional)
1 cup garbanzo beans (optional)
3 tablespoons beer or vodka (optional)
Salt to taste
3 pounds medium (26–30 count) fresh shrimp, peeled and deveined

---

Squeeze the lime juice into a large bowl; add sugar. Slice the onions into the thinnest rings possible and cut the "rings" into quarters. Put sliced onions in a strainer and run scalding hot tap water over them for 3 minutes. Immediately immerse them in the lime juice and allow the onions to marinate for 15 minutes.

Add all of the remaining ingredients, including the shrimp, always tasting as you go and making adjustments if you desire. Season with a pinch of salt. Refrigerate the ceviche for at least 2 hours (ideally, it is best to make it an entire day ahead of time), and sample it again before serving to see if it needs anything more.

Before serving, transfer to a decorative serving bowl, garnish with corn nuts and plantain chips or bread for dipping, and serve chilled with a case of ice-cold beer. Cures 12 hangovers.

## KETCHUP HEAVEN

If you fancy yourself a ketchup connoisseur, you must dip into a copy of Andrew F. Smith's magnum opus, *Pure Ketchup: A History of America's National Condiment.* Wade with him through oceans of ketchup, from apricot ketchup to anchovy catsup, leaving no bottle unopened. And you thought you knew your ketchup.

With all respect to Heinz™—the King of Ketchup—you'll be intrigued by the likes of Yours Truly Catsup™, Apollo Tomato Ketchup™, Ass Kickin' Ketchup™, Sailor Boy Ketchup™, Bug Catsup™, and Love Apple Ketchup™. And to balance the score, for every flask of Duchess Tomato Ketchup™, there is an honorary bottle of Knighthood Tomato Ketchup™ waiting to be opened.

# Eat for Pleasure

Do you eat the foods you love—and I mean really *love*—at every reasonable chance? Or do you just scarf down what you can, when you can, with little regard for taste and sensation? Do you eat for pleasure, or do you annihilate your meals with urgency? If food has become merely fast-lane fuel, it's high time to s-l-o-w down and relish the food that makes your soul sing more often and more consciously (think *Italia*). As you eat your way to vigor and glee, savor words of Peter Perkins, a.k.a. Cayenne Pete, epicure in the flow:

> My love and passion for eating stems from a quotation I have carried for decades, spoken by my inimitable teacher and mentor Marshall G. Pratt: "I eat for my pleasure, not effect, I hope." I find that the texture of foods combined with flavors and color are delightful to experiment with. I offer here a stunningly sensuous, yet texturally manly, recipe that I learned as a kitchen minion at the Lodge Club at Snowbird, Utah, and have prepared with love and total success for all these years since. So, just keep this in mind, and thank you for playing.

*Always preheat—then have fun.*

—June Saraceno

## Peter's Phyllo-Wrapped Gulf Prawns
### à la Lodge Club

16 prawns (about 1 pound), peeled,
  deveined, and halved, lengthwise
¾ cup (1½ sticks) clarified butter
1 cup Gruyere or pungent Swiss-like
  cheese, grated
1 cup Canadian bacon or smoked
  ham or turkey, finely diced

¼ cup capers, chopped
One 16-ounce package phyllo dough
  pastry sheets (use a good Greek
  brand)

---

Prepare the "nice fat shrimp" and clarify the butter (see page 61 for directions). Mix the cheese, meat, and capers together in a small bowl.

Preheat oven to 350°F. Lay out the phyllo sheets and cover with a cloth. Pulling three sheets at a time, lay the phyllo on a flat surface, longer side of the rectangular sheet toward you ("landscape view"), and coat the top sheet liberally with clarified butter.

Cut the sheet into 6 rectangular pieces (3 pieces, vertically, by 2 pieces, horizontally). Lay a sliced prawn near the lower corner of each phyllo rectangle, with the convex side (where the vein was) facing out from the center of each phyllo piece.

Drop about 1 tablespoon of the Swiss-meat-caper filling on the inside of the prawn. Twist up the phyllo loosely to form a tapered cone, with the prawn and filling encased at one end and taper at the other end. ("Phyllo has attitude," says Cayenne

Pete. "The trick is developing a knack for twisting them up into nice, elongated 'cones.'") Place the "cones" on an ungreased baking sheet and brush with more butter.

Bake for approximately 12 minutes or until the wrapped prawns are nicely browned. Serve on a bed of greens, accompanied by teriyaki-type dipping sauce, perhaps a little wasabi, and a lemon wedge and parsley for a garnish. They freeze beautifully if you want an excellent "prepare ahead" appetizer. Makes 6 manly appetizers.

> *Why is food so sexy?*
> *Sexual hunger and physical hunger*
> *have always been allies.*

—Diane Ackerman, *Natural History of the Senses*

# Fantasies of a Well-Fed Man

All men who love food should have a copy of *Newman's Own Cookbook* gracing their culinary libraries . . . or at least their kitchen counters. It is a lively romp through Paul Newman's and pal A. E. Hotchner's gastronomic universe, a "Best of" anthology full of fun ramblings about favorite foods and some darn good recipes to boot!

And Paul tells all. He tells us his deepest secrets and most profound dreams ("My salad dressing is literally something I dreamed up, the main part of it during a long night's sleep; the adjustments came in short afternoon naps"), and he tells us what turns him on about Caroline Murphy, the "other" woman in his life. . . . Caroline Murphy's Ham Hocks and Beans ("Here's the recipe . . . I would kill for"), Caroline Murphy's Tuna Salad ("unmatched . . . one of my favorites . . . our housekeeper's triumph"), and Caroline's Southern-Fried Chicken ("out of this world").

But have no doubt: It is his beloved co-star in his Academy Award-winning Screenplay of Life, wife and actress Joanne Woodward, who holds the key to his happiness—or at least to the bliss of his tastebuds. Of her Sole Cabernet, Cool Hand Cassidy (a.k.a. Paul Newman) proudly declares, "This is at the top of my list of favorite dishes. It is in a class by itself."

# Joanne Woodward's Sole Cabernet

4 tablespoons unsalted butter
4 fillets of sole (2 to 2½ pounds)
Salt and freshly ground pepper to
  taste

2 shallots, chopped
2 cups good cabernet sauvignon
1 cup Joanne's Hollandaise Sauce
  (recipe follows)

---

Preheat the oven to 375°F.

Put dabs of butter on the fillets of sole and fold them over crosswise. Add the salt, pepper, and shallots. Place in a baking pan and add the cabernet sauvignon. Bake for 10 minutes, then remove the fish to a plate.

Pour the wine sauce into a saucepan and reduce to ⅓ the original amount. Let cool. Add Joanne's Hollandaise Sauce to the wine sauce. Return the sole and sauce to the baking pan. Place in the oven for 5 minutes before serving. Make 4 servings.

---

# Joanne's Hollandaise Sauce

3 egg yolks
3 tablespoons cold water
1 stick (8 tablespoons) lightly salted
  butter, melted

Freshly ground pepper to taste
Juice of ½ lemon

123

Place the egg yolks and water in the top of a double boiler over hot but not boiling water. Whisk rapidly until the mixture thickens and an instant-read thermometer registers 160°F. Remove from the heat. Add the butter, little by little, while continuing to whisk. Add the pepper. Add the lemon juice just before serving. Makes 2 cups.

*A wise man always eats well.*

—Chinese proverb

# Kathy Is a **Catch**

All you single, hungry men out there, listen up—Kathy's cooking. Not only can this girl reel in her own fish and fry it up in a pan, she's also been known to climb a few mountains, run a dozen or so marathons, and have breakfast in Brazil and dinner in San Francisco— on the same day. And, she can definitely bait her own hook.

When I asked my free-spirited friend to share a typical meal she'd cook for a man, this is what she shot back. She insists that a self-caught fresh rainbow will enhance all aspects of this meal and added, "It is not always what you cook but the mood and tone you set. . . . Are the candles lit? Is his favorite drink chilling or on ice? . . . Start with an appetizer to keep him interested and focused. Then fix his favorite food!"

Guaranteed, Kathy's Fresh Catch will bring out the adventurous Boy Scout in you, and you will smile all the way to dessert.

*If one wished to be perfectly sincere,*
*one would have to admit there are two kinds of love—*
*well-fed and ill-fed. The rest is pure fiction.*

—Colette

# $\mathcal{K}$athy's Fresh Catch

4 tablespoons butter

1 small onion, sliced

4 cloves garlic

4 medium radishes

Two 12- to 14-ounce (pan-sized)
  whole fresh rainbow trout, scaled
  and gutted

Salt and pepper

---

In a large sauté pan, sauté the onions, garlic, and radishes in butter over medium heat for a minute or two. Reduce heat to low, put a cover on the pan, and cook the vegetables for 3 to 4 minutes, until *al dente*.

Add the prepared trout to the pan and cook on each side for 5 minutes (more or less, depending on the size of the fish). Season with salt and pepper. Makes 2 servings.

*Love is supreme and unconditional;*
*Like is nice, but limited.*

—Duke Ellington

# If Seafood Be the **Food** *of* **Love** . . .

Gentlemen, since we're on the topic, do you prefer it quick and zesty, or languid and luxurious? Wet and wild, you say? I'm talking about your food . . . your food, guys—remember, f-o-o-d. As you see, Aphrodite has struck again—the enchantress of the palate has waltzed into your mind with a seductive platter of her marquis seafood, and you start thinking about s-e-x.

Have you ever noticed how all of your senses are heightened when you eat a meal electricity-free, save the currents in your clothes? When you are nestled tête-à-tête with a paramour, accompanied only by candlelight, starlight, and moonlight, food rituals acquire a deliciously untamed quality. You feed each other with *all* your fingers and drink champagne straight from the bottle. Dining in the dark, quietly, candle flickering, gives an entirely new meaning to foreplay. Forget the "Clean Plate Club." It's time to make love for dessert.

With these two recipes, infused with practical aphrodisiacs, from scallops, mushrooms, and an otherworldly sauce to scampi and champagne, you'll be able to "live up to legend" on a nightly basis. Go Lothario!

# Mandarin Scallops Stir Fry

3 tablespoons grape seed oil

1 tablespoon butter

4 to 6 ounces shiitake mushrooms, sliced

1 tablespoon honey

2 pounds bay scallops

3 tablespoons Weir's Otherworld Wok Sauce™

1 teaspoon soy sauce

½ teaspoon pure vanilla extract

One 8-ounce can (1 cup) mandarin orange segments, juice strained, sliced in half lengthwise

1 tablespoon fresh parsley, minced

---

In a wok or the largest sauté pan in the house, heat the oil and butter to the smoking point. Add the mushrooms and stir for 1 minute. Drizzle the honey over the scallops, add them to the wok, and stir for 2 minutes or until golden.

Sprinkle Otherworld Wok Sauce, soy sauce, and vanilla over the scallops; keep stirring and frying. (To procure Weir's Otherworld Wok Sauce, the key ingredient, see page 212 of Red Letter Resources.) Finally, add the mandarin orange segments and stir-fry for 2 more minutes. Remove from heat and sprinkle with fresh parsley. Serve immediately with steamed white rice. Makes 4 servings.

*After sexual comportment or orientation,*
*food is for us the greatest measure of self.*

—Nigella Lawson

# $S$*parkling* $S$*campi in* $M$*ascarpone* $C$*ream* $S$*auce*

2 to 3 garlic cloves, pressed
2 tablespoons extra-virgin olive oil
4 tablespoons butter
¾ cup dry sherry
1½ cups half-and-half
8 ounces mascarpone cheese
Salt and pepper

2 teaspoons extra-virgin olive oil
1 pound scampi or jumbo prawns,
   shelled and deveined
1 cup Asti Spumante or other dry
   sparkling wine
Parmigiano Reggiano and Romano
   cheeses, grated together

---

In a large sauté pan over medium-high heat, sauté the garlic in olive oil for a minute or two until the garlic begins to bronze. Reduce heat to medium and add the butter, gently sautéing the garlic for 2 to 3 minutes more. Add the sherry and let the mixture reduce for 2 to 3 minutes more, until slightly thickened.

Reduce heat to low and add half-and-half and mascarpone, stirring to blend well. (Watch the heat, because if it is too hot, the sauce will break; keep the sauce just below the boiling point.) Add a splash of sherry and salt and pepper according to taste.

In the meanwhile, sauté the prawns in olive oil in another pan over medium-high heat for 2 to 3 minutes. Reduce heat to medium, add sparkling wine, and sauté until the prawns begins to curl (about 3 minutes). Turn them over and cook for 3 more minutes, checking for tenderness with a fork. Turn off heat and leave the pan on burner.

Pour the cream sauce over the prawns, stir slightly, and let flavors meld for a few minutes. Serve with fettuccine or rice, Steamed Sesame Asparagus (recipe follows), and a sprinkle of a mixture of Parmigiano Reggiano and Romano cheeses. Makes 4 servings.

# *S*teamed *S*esame *A*sparagus

| | |
|---|---|
| 1 pound tender asparagus | 2 teaspoons butter |
| 1 cup water | 2 teaspoons sesame seeds |
| 2 garlic cloves, sliced | Sesame oil |
| ¼-inch fresh ginger root, sliced | Salt and pepper |

Cut off and discard the tough ends of the asparagus spears. In a large saucepan, mix the water, garlic, and ginger root and bring to a boil. Steam the asparagus over this broth for 5 to 7 minutes until tender.

Meanwhile, in a large sauté pan, toast the sesame seeds in butter over medium heat. Add a few dashes of sesame oil. Set aside until the spears are cooked.

Transfer the steamed asparagus spears to the sauté pan with the sesame seeds. Roll the stalks around a bit to coat with seeds, season to taste, and serve. Makes 4 servings.

---

**HOLY DISH, BATMAN!**

The saints are marching in, favorite offerings in hand. Have you ever tried St. Peter's Fish—the tilapia—with its sweet, fine-textured taste? Excellent for baking, broiling, grilling, and steaming. Try it with a bowl of *Saint-Germain*, a nice, thick, fresh pea soup, and give praise afterward for *Saint-Honoré*, a heavenly dessert like you've never known.

# Calling **K**londike **K**ate

When you walk into a bar and see a sign that reads "Leave Your Firearms with the Bartender," you're definitely not at the Bubble Lounge in Manhattan. Welcome to the land of the Iditarod, grizzlies, and mosquitoes as big as hummingbirds. Where women are scarce and men are starving. . . .

Not for food, however; the coastline is brimming with salmon. According to an article in *GQ*, "Despite the legendary madams like Klondike Kate . . . Alaskan men outnumber women forty to one. To lure women from near and far to the forsaken snowdrifts, the Talkeetna Bachelor Society throws an annual auction." This bacchanalian "auction," where men do the full monty while the babes go wild "bidding" for them and their services, gives a new meaning to "Baked Alaska." As the T-shirts say, "The Odds Are Good, But the Goods Are Odd."

What will she do when she "wins" her backwoods stud? Doubtful she'll cook for him. But if she does, it'll be moose, halibut, or salmon . . . and it will be wild.

*Conversation is the enemy of food and good wine.*

—Alfred Hitchcock

# Wild Alaska Honey-Lime Salmon

| | |
|---|---|
| 1 pound fresh Pacific salmon fillet | 2 tablespoons extra-virgin olive oil |
| Kosher salt and black pepper, freshly milled | 2 tablespoons butter |
| | 2 tablespoons of honey |
| ¼ cup unbleached flour | Juice of 1 lime |

Preheat the oven to 450°F. Cut the salmon into two equal pieces; season with salt and pepper to taste. Melt the butter and honey together in a small saucepan over low heat or in the microwave. Add the lime juice and blend well. Set aside.

Sprinkle the flour on a large plate. Lightly dredge both sides of the fish through the flour. In large pan, heat the olive oil to the smoking point over medium-high heat. Fry the salmon, skin side down, for 2 to 3 minutes; gently flip and cook the other side for approximately 3 minutes more, or until golden brown; it should be slightly undercooked.

Transfer the fish to a large, lightly oiled baking dish, skin side down. Lather it with the honey-lime marinade and bake, uncovered, for 7 to 10 minutes (until the fish is slightly pink in the center). Makes 2 servings.

# A Dish Fit for a **King** ... or a **Fireman**

Years ago, I came across an article about the Balearic Islands off the Catalan coast of Spain—Ibiza, Majorca, and Minorca are the most well known—and I've been obsessed ever since. Not with the islands, but with a stew called *caldereta de langosta,* a Minorcan masterpiece of fish, shellfish, and lobster. This trophy dish is the rage at Es Pla restaurant. Just ask King Juan Carlos of Spain; he's a regular.

My search for an authentic recipe for calderata de langosta, a distant, distant cousin to cioppino, took me to gourmet hunting grounds *everywhere,* including the unlikely lair of some unsuspecting gumshoe gourmets, the San Francisco firemen. While the debate raged on whether the cioppino originated in the Golden Gate City (claim the firemen) or in Liguria, Italy (insists Mario Batali), my coveted caldereta evaded me. So I gathered about twenty recipes for cioppino, bouillabaisse, Catalonian shellfish stew—you name it—and put some great minds and taste buds to work. I offer a true culinary *tour de force*—the Stew of the Seven Seas. Let the mermaids spoon-feed you all the way to Atlantis. . . .

> *Many men go fishing all of their lives without*
> *knowing that it is not fish they are after.*
>
> —Henry David Thoreau

🐟 133

# *C*aldereta del **M**ar

One 1- to 1½-pound lobster or three
  large lobster tails
1¼ pounds (10 to 12) clams, washed
  and scrubbed
1¼ pounds (14 to 16) mussels,
  washed and scrubbed
1 pound large prawns (16 to 20),
  peeled and deveined, tail shell
  attached
8 ounces sea scallops, cut in half
8 ounces halibut, cut into 1-inch cubes
8 ounces cod fillet, cut into 1-inch
  cubes
⅓ cup extra-virgin olive oil
4 garlic cloves, roughly chopped
1 medium red onion, chopped
1 green bell pepper, seeded and
  chopped

1 red bell pepper, seeded and
  chopped
1¼ cup dry white wine
Two 28-ounce cans whole peeled
  tomatoes, coarsely chopped with
  all juice
1 teaspoon kosher salt
½ teaspoon dried thyme
½ teaspoon dried oregano
2 bay leaves
¼ teaspoon saffron
Juice of ½ lemon
More water, if needed
¼ cup Italian parsley, coarsely
  chopped
¼ cup fresh basil, coarsely chopped
Salt and freshly ground pepper

---

Prepare the lobster (see The Inside Line on next page) and other shellfish and
set aside.

In a heavy-bottomed pot or Dutch oven, heat the olive until smoking over medium heat. Add the garlic, onion, and peppers and sauté until they are soft and golden, about 5 to 7 minutes. Add the wine, tomatoes, salt, thyme, oregano, bay leaves, and saffron and bring to a boil, stirring thoroughly.

Add the lobster, clams, and mussels, cover, and bring to a boil; cook for 2 to 3 minutes. Then reduce heat to medium-low, add the shrimp, scallops, halibut, cod, and lemon juice and simmer, covered, for 15 to 20 minutes more, until most of the clams and mussels have opened (discard any clams or mussels that do not open in "due" time). Add some water if the stew is too thick, sprinkle with the parsley and basil, and season with salt and pepper as desired.

Serve right out of the cauldron, accompanied by the best bread you can find, grilled or toasted. Makes 4 hearty servings.

## THE INSIDE LINE

To prepare the lobster for the cauldron, kill it humanely by inserting the tip of a large knife (point aimed lengthwise) into the point where the head and body meet. With a cleaver or large knife, chop off the tail section of the lobster at the point where it joins the body and then cut the tail crosswise into 1-inch thick slices. Twist or cut off the large claws, and cut the body of the lobster in half lengthwise. Discard the gelatinous sac in the head and the whitish vein attached to it, but leave the greenish brown substance (the liver) and black roe, if there is any (enhances flavor). Yum. Any hesitation, just buy lobster tails and slice them, shells on, into medallions.

*Life itself is the proper binge.*

—Julia Child

# Magnificent
# Meat and
# Potatoes

What is universal is the primal pleasure we take in feeding our faces—and in the process, our souls.

—Autumn Stephens,
*Wild Women in the Kitchen*

## Sizzling Secrets of a Satisfied Man

HE LOVES . . .

 **A** great beef bourguignonne with attitude.—*John, Nevada*

**A** killer pork chop from Lark Creek Inn and scalloped potatoes.—*Jay, California*

**A** four-bone prime rib blackened on the outside, medium rare on the inside. Seasoning? Never touch a fine piece of meat—sacrilege!
—*J. E. Ricketts, Wisconsin*

**L**amb chops—medium rare—mashed potatoes with white horseradish, and a good Chianti.—*Michael, Nevada*

**E**xtreme surf and turf . . . fresh venison and ahi medallions pan-fried in garlic, whiskey, and wine over extreme heat.—*Jeff, California*

## To Thine Own **Stew** Be True

Every *bona fide* meat-loving man out there eating his way through life should find a kick-ass recipe for what I call "meat and potatoes in motion"—a bold and hearty beef stew recipe that really satisfies the urgings of stomach and soul—and stick with it. Then he can leisurely spend his days perfecting his recipe, cooking it up as often as desired. It will make him a happy man.

Great men knew great stews. Eisenhower loved an old-fashioned Burgundy beef stew with small Irish potatoes that enjoyed a truly *grand* reputation; Mamie's original recipe calls for twenty pounds of meat and serves sixty people (and that was the least amount she would bother making). Ronald Reagan's favorite Truckadero Beef Stew is a spectacle with artichoke hearts, mushrooms, and Burgundy, and Burt Reynolds jazzes up his Burt's Beef Stew with bacon, carrots, and a few dashes of MSG. Even the legendary Liberace relied on his Burgundy Beef Valentino, made with lean sirloin, pearl onions, and butter, to keep his fingers keen on the keys.

When not working his magic at Guastavino's in New York City, Executive Chef Daniel Orr loves making his signature stew at home for friends. Consider yourself his friend—this bold and hearty carnivore's dream meal certainly outdoes itself.

# $\mathcal{G}$*uastavino's* **C***uban* **T***ripe* **S***tew*

2 pounds tripe, cut into ½-inch strips,
   rinsed well in cold water for 1 hour
Lightly salted water
2 tablespoons olive oil
1 pound pork spare ribs (4 ribs),
   seasoned with salt and pepper
One ¾-pound smoked ham hock
4 oxtail pieces
6 cloves garlic
1 large Spanish onion, thinly sliced
½ bottle white wine (approximately
   1¾ cups)
One 28-ounce can crushed tomatoes
   with juice

2 thyme branches
2 bay leaves
¼ teaspoon crushed red pepper flakes
1 pound spicy dried chorizo sausage,
   cut into ½-inch, angled slices
½ pound dried baby lima beans,
   prepared
1 large Idaho potato, peeled, diced
   into large cubes
Salt and pepper
1 fresh tomato, diced
½-bunch fresh cilantro or Italian
   parsley, roughly chopped

---

Place tripe in a large pot, cover with salted water, and bring to a boil over medium-high heat. Reduce heat to low and simmer for 30 to 45 minutes, until tripe begins to become tender. Remove from heat, drain hot water, and rinse the tripe with cold water. Set aside.

In a large pot over high heat, sear the seasoned spareribs, ham hock, and oxtails in olive oil until nicely caramelized. Add the garlic and sauté it until it begins to brown. Then add the onions and cook for 3 to 5 minutes. When the onions are translucent, add the tripe, white wine, tomatoes, thyme, bay, and crushed pepper and stir together.

After bringing the contents to a boil, reduce heat to low and simmer for 1½ to 2 hours, until the tripe is very tender. (Orr coaches, "It is very important that the tripe is tender and that the potatoes are perfectly cooked; without this the dish is flawed.")

Meanwhile, rinse the lima beans and simmer in a pot of water over low heat until tender (follow package directions). Season with salt and pepper.

After the stew has cooked and the tripe is tender, add the sausage, beans, and potatoes and cook for an additional 30 minutes, until the potatoes are tender. Season to taste. (*Note:* The stew can be made to this point and chilled. Skim off any excess fat that surfaces before reheating and adjust seasoning if desired.) Serve at once in large bowls garnished with diced tomatoes and fresh cilantro. Makes 4 generous servings.

## THE INSIDE LINE

In the event your taste buds and your uninitiated imagination are reluctant to try tripe, just omit it until you're feeling a bit bolder. Adjust the directions accordingly and add some beef and burgundy while you're at it!

This stew, inspired by a meal that Chef Orr enjoys at a Cuban restaurant in Chelsea on his days off, is actually even better when reheated. Just divide into batches and freeze; it's best to leave the potatoes out until reheating.

# Go for the **Bold**

A girlfriend with whom I trade recipes recently confessed, "By the way, my husband, Larry, who was seduced with Fettuccine Alfredo, *loves* your meatloaf. We have it once a week, and he'd eat it three or four nights in a row if he could!" What a compliment! It's true—men do love meatloaf. A quintessential American comfort food, it ranks high with mac and cheese and tuna noodle casserole. (It seemed like they ate it on *Father Knows Best* and *Mayberry RFD* every episode.) Harry Truman adored it; Nancy Reagan made sure Ronnie was served his favorite roast beef hash on Sunday nights, always well done.

Look no further for the recipe of ages. If you make it, go for the glory with all the trimmings. The "spirits" and Heinz ketchup clinches the gold-medal taste, and Shivani's Outrageous Potatoes (recipe follows), a "truly organic endeavor," give this meal a life of its own.

*My doctor told me to stop having intimate dinners for four.*
*Unless there are three other people.*

—Orson Welles

# The Magnificent Meatloaf

**The Loaf**

1½ pounds premium ground beef,
  your choice

1 small onion, finely chopped

¼ cup fresh parsley, finely chopped

2 to 3 cloves garlic, minced

1 cup quick oats, uncooked

1 egg

¼ cup sweet relish or chutney

½ cup Heinz ketchup

2 teaspoons dry leaf oregano

1 teaspoon salt

1 teaspoon curry powder

1 teaspoon paprika

¼ teaspoon ground cinnamon

10 to 12 dashes hot pepper sauce
  (Tabasco and Weir's Snake Oil Hot
  Sauce are my favorites)

**Topping**

1 to 2 tablespoons beer, wine, or
  whiskey (optional, but it is the
  "secret")

Additional ketchup

Few dashes of hot pepper sauce

1 tablespoon brown sugar

2 tablespoons fresh Parmesan cheese,
  grated

Salt and cracked black pepper

---

Preheat oven to 350°F. In a large bowl, combine all of the "loaf" ingredients by hand (I mean *literally;* just get in there and "goosh" it up with clean hands). Grease a 9 x 5-inch loaf pan or special meatloaf pan (reduces oil) and fill with the meat mixture, patting and rounding the top.

Sprinkle the top of the loaf evenly with your booze of choice (I like beer). Next, lather on more ketchup and sprinkle with hot sauce, brown sugar, and Parmesan (in that order). Season with a shake of salt and cracked black pepper and bake uncovered for 1 hour. Serves 2 to 4 hungry men (and probably 6 average eaters).

# *Shivani's Outrageous Potatoes*

6 large russet potatoes, unpeeled

Two 10¾-ounce cans "cream of something" soup (mushroom, chicken, or celery)

16-ounce tub sour cream

½ cup (1 stick) butter, melted

1½ cups cheddar cheese, grated

1 small bunch green onions, chopped

2 teaspoons garlic powder

Salt and pepper

In a large pan, boil the potatoes in their skins in slightly salted water until they are tender when pierced with a fork (about 20 to 25 minutes). When done, run cool water over the potatoes and peel them. Slice potatoes into pieces.

Preheat the oven to 350°F. In a large mixing bowl, combine all other ingredients. Season to taste with salt and pepper. Fold in potatoes. Turn the outrageous mixture into a buttered 1½-quart glass or ceramic baking dish. Bake uncovered for 30 to 35 minutes, until the potatoes get bubbly and turn a golden brown. Makes 6 MMMMMMMMMMmmmmmmmmmmmmmGOOD!!!!!!!!!!! servings.

*She had no idea how magical, how reassuring,*
*how pleasurable her simple meat loaf was for me,*
*what a delight even lumpy mashed potatoes were. . . .*

—Anthony Bourdain, *Kitchen Confidential*

## IRISH EYES ARE ON MOM'S COOKING

Forty years ago, David Simon, Ph.D., then a high school student in Sycamore, Illinois, interviewed his school's football team about the foods they loved. Every player on the team said, "Steak," except one, who said he loved "Tapioca."

I had the privilege of asking the 2000 Notre Dame Fighting Irish football team to share their dream meals and tell me the foods they ate to shore up their scrimmages. Behold the foodstuff of champions:

"Pizza, Powerade™, and ribs." —*Jim Molinaro, offensive tackle*

"Steak, steak, steak . . . chocolate cake." —*Rocky Boiman, outside linebacker*

"XL pizza with extra cheese and all the meats and a big glass of lemonade." —*Jeffrey Faine, center*

"Shrimp Alfredo and Gatorade™." —*Gary Godsey, tight end*

"Lasagna." —*David Givens, wide receiver*

"Ribs . . . Mom's cooking . . ." —*Javin Hunter, wide receiver*

# Bonnie Knows the Recipe
## to **Every Man's Heart**

During my heyday as the original baker and *strudel-frau,* anyone who was anyone would take their lunch break at Bonnie's while skiing on Ajax Mountain in Aspen, Colorado. The line-up at this cafeteria-style restaurant was like the red carpet procession at the Academy Awards or the Inaugural Ball. On any given day, Jack Nicholson would load up his tray with soups and desserts, and the entire Kennedy clan would polish off the rest. (I wonder if Donald Trump got indigestion on the afternoon at Bonnie's when Ivana met Marla. . . .)

Bonnie Brucker Rayburn is Bonnie's class act; she always insisted every dish served was homemade, fresh, and dosed with a lot of heart and soul. Though she no longer regularly takes the chairlift to work with the rest of the crew, Bonnie is still something of a local legend, and the restaurant still carries her name. In the meantime, she's busy with her friends and family and, as always, cooking food with love that everyone loves.

Bonnie claims, "I've made a thousand pot roasts, and this is the one I always come back to. . . . Men love it." Add a spectacular *pomme de terre en robe de chamber* ("earth apple in its dressing gown," as the French say), a.k.a. dynamite baked potato, and you will know true satisfaction.

# $\mathcal{S}$lottsstek (**Swedish P**ot **R**oast)

2 tablespoons butter

2 tablespoons vegetable oil

3- to 4-pound chuck roast

1 cup onions, finely chopped

3 tablespoons flour

1 tablespoon dark Karo™ syrup

2 tablespoons champagne wine
   vinegar or white wine vinegar

2 cups beef stock (Bonnie likes
   Minor's™)

1 large bay leaf

6 flat anchovy filets, washed, dried,
   and diced

Freshly ground black pepper to taste

Salt

---

Preheat the oven to 325°F. In a heavy 5- to 6-quart pot (prefers cast iron), melt butter with oil over moderate heat. When foam subsides, add the meat and brown it on all sides. Remove meat from pot and set aside.

Add chopped onions to the pot and cook over moderate heat for 6 to 8 minutes, until they are lightly browned, stirring occasionally. Remove pan from heat and add flour, stirring gently to dissolve. Pour in Karo syrup, vinegar, and beef stock. Add bay leaf, anchovies, and freshly ground pepper.

Return meat to the pot, cover, and bring to a boil on top of the stove. Then place the pot in the lower third of the oven and cook for approximately 3 hours (check the pot each hour and add extra water if necessary). When done, the meat should be very tender and offer no resistance.

You can also add unpeeled, quartered red potatoes and some peeled and quartered carrots for the last hour of cooking. Then you will have a full meal in one dish! Makes 6 to 8 servings. *Bon appetit!*

## The **Regal Roasted** *Russet*

1 large 8- to 12-ounce russet or Idaho
   potato in its "dressing gown"
Extra-virgin olive oil
Sea salt

Butter
Sour cream
Fresh chives, chopped
Salt and pepper

---

Preheat the oven to 350°F. Scrub the spud, pat it dry, anoint it with olive oil, and rub it with salt. Place it on a baking sheet in the center of the oven and bake for 1½ hours.

When the potato is hot out of the oven, slit the top, lengthwise, with a sharp knife. Season with salt and pepper and stuff the potato with a couple slices of butter. Finally, crown your creation with a dollop of sour cream sprinkled with chives. Makes 1 perfectly roasted, regal russet.

*Throughout my life friends and fortune have*
*come and gone but I've always been able to*
*count on a baked potato to see me through.*

—Maggie Waldron

# When Life Gives You *Lemons* . . . Make **Beer!**

Mark Twain once said, "The secret to life is making your vocation your vacation." What a dream. Some of us have done it; few of us do, but it remains such a delicious thought. . . .

Once upon a time, my friend Fred Strachan toiled in the rat race of Silicon Valley for twelve long years. Then one day, the gods of the recession descended upon him and bestowed the dreaded condition upon him: layoff. Fred, concerned for his ladylove and their young child, asked for a sign.

Maybe it was those strong Strachan German genes or maybe it was the Fates, but the heavens opened and the little voices said, "Go to beer school." So Fred commuted hundreds and hundreds of miles, four hours a day, to the University of California at Davis, where one day, he was magically transformed into a brewmaster. As happy endings go, Brewmaster Fred was rewarded with a job at Sierra Nevada Brewing Company in the mecca of microbreweries: Chico, California. He now produces the finest ales in the world and plays with his wife, Susan, and two Fredlets every chance he gets.

And the vacation part? Fred sailed off to the World Brewing Congress near Walt Disney World in Orlando one summer. No, it wasn't a stout-induced hallucination; the world's finest brewers were all there swimming in suds.

*For a quart of ale is a dish for a king.*

—Shakespeare, *The Winter's Tale*

# Pork *C*hops in Stout

½ cup flour

Salt and pepper

1 tablespoon unsalted butter

2 tablespoons extra-virgin olive oil, divided

4 center loin pork chops, cut 1 inch thick

3 large onions, thinly sliced

3 cloves garlic, minced

1 cup stout, divided

1 cup chicken stock, divided

1 tablespoon coarse mustard

1 tablespoon fresh parsley, chopped

1½ teaspoons balsamic vinegar

---

Sprinkle the flour in a shallow container and season with salt and pepper. Melt the butter and 1 tablespoon of oil in a large skillet over medium-high heat. Dredge the chops in flour, place in the skillet, and brown on each side. Remove them from the heat and set aside in the skillet.

Transfer the leftover flour to a paper bag, add the onions, and shake together.

In the same skillet you used to brown the chops, heat 1 tablespoon of olive oil over medium heat, add the floured onions, and sauté for 1 minute. Add the garlic, season with salt, and cook for 5 minutes, covered, stirring once. Uncover and cook for 3 to 4 minutes more, stirring occasionally.

Deglaze the skillet with ¾ cup stout and ¾ cup chicken stock and return the chops to the pan, spooning the onions over them. Add the remaining stout and stock, enough to bring the liquid level halfway up the sides of the pork chops. Cover and simmer for 20 minutes. Turn pork over and cook until tender, about 25 minutes. Transfer the chops and onions to a serving dish and keep warm.

Remove excess grease from the sauce left in the skillet and simmer the remaining sauce over medium-low heat for about 10 minutes. Whisk in the mustard, parsley, and vinegar and season with salt and pepper to taste. Blanket the pork chops with the stout sauce and serve. Makes 4 servings.

*Good potatoes,*
*Good meat,*
*Good God, let's eat!*

—My dad's favorite "grace"

# German Home-Fried New Potatoes

2 pounds marble-sized new red
  potatoes, prepared
1 tablespoon extra-virgin olive oil

2 tablespoons butter
2 garlic cloves, finely chopped
1 tablespoon fresh parsley, chopped

---

After cleaning the potatoes, either prick each with a fork and microwave on HIGH for 5 minutes or boil in water, unpricked, for 10 to 12 minutes. Cut the potatoes in half, lengthwise.

In a large sauté pan over medium-high heat, melt the butter in the olive oil with the garlic. Add the potatoes and sauté for 4 to 5 minutes; nudge the potatoes about the pan as they sauté.

Lower the heat to medium and continuing frying the potatoes for about 10 more minutes, covered, shaking the pan occasionally until they are golden brown and firm but tender. Sprinkle the parsley over them in the pan, stir, and serve. Makes 4 servings.

*There's Something About*

# Mary's Little Lamb

I have to apologize. I don't eat lamb. So when swarms of men told me that the food they love above all others is lamb, I was shocked. Lamb? Though the general masses of men worship at the Temple of the T-Bone, and many of their brethren give praise to the Venerable Veal and Pontificated Pork, there is a huge undercurrent of pilgrims headed for the Land of Lamb, meat lovers who weaken in awe at the thought of a succulent lamb shank, a barbecued leg of lamb, or a huge plate of darling, delectable lamb chops.

Even their wives don't know they love lamb. After a gentleman friend told me he would definitely order lamb chops as his last meal, I asked his wife (of fifteen years) if she had a good recipe. "What? What do you mean he likes lamb chops? I never knew that!" I felt like I was caught having a secret affair with him.

Another friend, journalist and author Robert Frohlich, shared an exquisite story called "Lamb for Lovers" about a woman he loved, who one evening cooked an unforgettable dinner of lamb shanks, salad, and a chocolate-tangerine tart. Just the thought still soothes his senses to this day. And so I learned . . . men's love for lamb, a sincere and simple love, is rooted deeply in their epicurean souls . . . and this is a beautiful thing.

# Honey-Rosemary Lamb Chops

8 lamb loin chops, cut ½-inch thick
3 garlic cloves, 1 crushed and 2 thinly
  sliced
1 teaspoon dried rosemary

2 to 3 tablespoons extra-virgin
  olive oil, divided
⅔ cup honey
Rosemary, salt, and pepper

---

Rub the lamb chops with the crushed garlic and the rosemary. Mix 1 tablespoon of olive oil with the honey. Using a pastry brush or small spatula, "paint" the chops with the honey mixture. Let stand, covered, at room temperature for 45 minutes to an hour.

Heat the remaining olive oil and sliced garlic in a large sauté pan over medium-high heat. (*Note:* You may need two pans; if so, just divide the oil and garlic evenly between the two.)

Add the lamb chops and sauté, turning once, for approximately 2 minutes on each side, until they are a golden brown but pink inside. Season with an additional pinch of rosemary and salt and pepper to taste. Serve immediately with a generous mound of Spiced Garlic Spuds topped with Great Crater Gravy (recipes follow). Makes 3 to 4 servings.

# *Spiced Garlic Spuds*

4 large Yukon Gold potatoes (about
  2 pounds), peeled and cut into large
  chunks
2 tablespoons butter
2 tablespoons mayonnaise

Juice from 3 pressed garlic cloves
¾ teaspoon cream horseradish sauce
½ cup whole milk, warmed
Salt and pepper

---

In a large saucepan, cover the potatoes with an extra inch of cold, lightly salted water and bring to a boil over high heat. Reduce heat to medium and cook, covered (leaving the lid askew on the pan to prevent potato-water eruptions), for 15 to 20 minutes until potatoes are tender when tested with a fork.

Drain the water and return the pan to the burner, *heat off* (the remaining heat will steam out excess moisture and reduce starchiness). Using a potato masher, mash the potatoes together with the butter, mayonnaise, garlic juice, horseradish sauce, and half of the warm milk. Slowly add the remaining milk, mashing until the potatoes are the desired texture. Season with salt and pepper to taste and then whip the spuds until they are smooth and creamy. Makes 4 servings.

# Great Crater Gravy

3 tablespoons butter
3 tablespoons flour
One 15-ounce can beef broth
One 10¾-ounce can cream of
  mushroom soup

¾ cup water
Salt and pepper

---

In a large saucepan over medium heat, blend the butter and flour until a golden brown roux forms. Whisk in the broth, a few tablespoons at a time, until the entire amount has been added. Reduce heat to low; add the mushroom soup and water and whisk all ingredients together.

Let the gravy simmer at a gentle boil, stirring gently, until it is nice and creamy. Serve in the craters of big mounds of mashed potatoes. Makes 4 servings.

*We offer a prayer for peace and grace and spiritual food,*
*For wisdom and guidance, for all these are good,*
*But don't forget the potatoes.*

—John Tyler Petter

## WHAT IS A MAN? A BEAST. NO MORE.
—Shakespeare, *Hamlet*

Even Thomas Jefferson kept the woods around Monticello stocked with wild game and his ponds and streams bursting with fish so that when he needed to "reconnect" with his manhood, he could hunt or fish. To one degree or another, the archetypal "return from the hunt" will always boast an essential role in a man's psyche.

Are you a weekend warrior returning home from a wilderness of business conquests to plunder the fridge? Or, have you returned from a stretch in the woods with a trophy buck that you took down with a bow and arrow and a year's supply of venison? To each his extreme.

My advice to all huntresses out there? When your beast returns from the "hunt," always let him open the pickle jar to show off his true strength.

# Eat Your Way Through the Blues

Homesick for home cooking? You are not alone. This nostalgia-drenched six-page, handwritten letter arrived from one gentleman:

What do men like to eat? I like to eat everything. Men like food their moms or grandmothers cooked; it's the way they cooked it. I like to cook and I like to eat—don't know which I like better.

In my hometown (Ellwood City, Pennsylvania) the Italians would start to make Sunday dinner on Friday and cook all through Saturday for supper after Mass on Sunday. Everything was homemade, from scratch. Back East, you didn't walk in the front door; you walked in the back door and the kitchen table was as far as you would get.

For the longest time, I thought everyone eats this way. I didn't go to a restaurant until I was in the service. You don't realize what good food is until you can't find it.

Rest assured, friend, with this recipe and its ethnic zest, you have found good food (and you won't need three days to fix it). Enjoy.

*I have discovered that there is romance in food*
*when romance has disappeared from everywhere else.*
*And as long as my digestion holds out,*
*I will follow romance.*

—Hemingway

157

# Spanish Veal with Almond Sauce

2 tablespoons extra-virgin olive oil

1 clove garlic, peeled

1 pound boneless veal, cut 1-inch thick, thinly sliced across the grain

¾ cup chicken broth

¼ cup sherry

1 teaspoon cornstarch

½ cup pimiento-stuffed olives, sliced

¼ cup blanched almonds, toasted and ground

---

Heat the oil and garlic clove in a wok or large sauté pan over high heat. When the garlic clove has browned in the oil, remove and discard it.

Add the veal slices, a few at a time, to the wok and stir-fry 1 to 2 minutes until lightly browned. Remove the veal and set aside; keep warm.

Add the broth to the wok, reduce heat to medium, and return all veal strips to the broth. Cover and simmer for 12 to 15 minutes, stirring occasionally. Add the sherry and the almonds. Cook, stirring, for 4 to 5 minutes, until the sauce thickens. Stir in the olives and season with salt and pepper. Serve over rice or noodles. Makes 4 to 6 servings.

# Playing with
# Fire

I find it hard to understand why someone would cook a steak any other way. . . . The succulent beauty of a grilled steak is one of the great pleasures of life.

—Derrick Riches, *about.com*

*Seeking Thrills with the G-r-r-r-ill*

HE LOVES . . .

**A**nything from the grill. There is nothing like having a beer while standing around the grill. It reminds me of my previous life as a caveman grilling wild boar ribs.—*Rit, New Jersey*

**H**ands-down, above all, my dad's peanut butter pork satay.—*Brandon, Indiana*

**G**rilled salmon patties with creamed asparagus.—*Uncle Dave, Illinois*

**B**BQ ribs smoked on my smoker with Rib Tickler™ sauce, eaten with Roy and friends and a huge frosty of microbrew.—*M. B. B., Nevada*

**F**lank steak grilled to medium on the Weber™, red "new" potatoes with lots of butter, corn on the cob, Budweiser™ long necks. . . . I do no work at all on this meal; my sexy wife does it all.—*Pat, Colorado*

# "Which Way Do I **Steer** for . . .

. . . a Cheeseburger in Paradise?" Just take a quick detour through Margaritaville and out to the barbecue pit. We're Q-in' now! Since man first rubbed his two sticks together and started the first fire—maybe five minutes afterward—there has been meat sizzling on the grill. Actually, it was the hot-blooded Spaniards who introduced *barbacoa* (named for the grid of sticks on which meat was roasted) in the Americas, a technique they learned from Caribbean Indians. Needless to say, men embraced this new food-worshiping religious practice, and the Church of the Almighty Grill—an offshoot of the First Church of the Holy Brew—sprung up in backyards and on patios around the country.

Membership in this congregation has mushroomed into the millions. Former converts included pit presidents Thomas Jefferson and Texan Lyndon B. Johnson, who helped make barbecues and parades cornerstones of good ol' red-blooded Americana. Today, the Reverend Jimmy Buffet writes the hymns, and televangelist-cum-grill guru Bobby Flay preaches the good word. Praise the fire gods! The coals are hot, the beers are cold, the mugs are frosty.

> *Don't make the mistake of using ground round or sirloin*
> *in this recipe; many hamburger cooks fall short of my standards*
> *because they use meat that is simply too good.*

—Paul Newman, *Newman's Own Cookbook*

# Hamburger du *P*aradis à Mourir
## *(Burger in Paradise to Die For)*

1 pound ground chuck
Kosher salt and freshly ground
   pepper
4 slices Gruyere cheese, thickly sliced
4 slices Cheddar cheese, thickly sliced
4 leaves romaine lettuce

1 large beefsteak tomato, sliced into
   ¼-inch slices
1 Vidalia or Bermuda onion, sliced
   into ¼-inch segments and grilled
   (optional)
4 top-shelf hamburger buns

---

Preheat the grill to high. Divide the meat into 4 burgers and season on both sides with salt and pepper. Cook for 3 to 4 minutes on each side (medium rare) over direct heat. (If using, brush the onions with a small amount of olive oil and grill while the burgers are cooking.)

When burgers are almost done, top the meat with a slice of each cheese. Split the buns and toast on the grill, cut side down. Cover the grill for a minute, until the cheese melts a bit. Assemble and serve with Heinz 57™, French-fried potatoes, a big kosher pickle, and a cold draft beer. Transports 2 to 4 men to Paradise.

## Rubbing Butts with the **S**tars

It's the hottest thing since Tabasco. You take a chicken, rub it with "dry rub," perch it on a can of beer—butt up—and slow cook it over a bed of coals. Everyone's doing the "beer butt chicken." Barbecue barons are winning Q-ing contests with it, gourmets are succumbing left and right to its succulent outcome, and stars like Matthew McConaughey are doing it on TV!

It's not rocket science—the rub tenderizes the meat, and the steam from the beer moistens it—but it does make a good conversation piece and keeps boredom at bay. Though it all seems oddly discourteous to the poor chicken, it really is an innovative means to a very tasty end and is a lot of fun on top of that.

This beauty of a butt, inspired by Matt's Texas Butt Chicken recipe, which he demo'd for the *Rosie O'Donnell Show,* is grand when polished off with Uncle Sven's Secret Sauce, a recipe invented by my friend's uncle during a wild weekend of Wesson™ oil parties at the University of Colorado years ago. Don't ask . . . just enjoy.

*The man with meat seeks fire.*

—Nigerian proverb

# **B**ravado **B**ud **B**utt *C*hicken

One 4-pound chicken (or larger)

2 tablespoons Lawry's™ Coarse
  Ground Garlic with Chopped Parsley

2 tablespoons Creole seasoning

1 can Budweiser™ (or other beer)

Uncle Sven's Secret Sauce (recipe
  follows)

---

The night before cooking, rinse the chicken thoroughly, removing extra skin and fat. Mix together the spices (see page 87 for Big Easy Creole Seasoning recipe or use a favorite store brand) and rub the chicken with seasoning inside and out, working well into the skin and under the skin where possible. Wrap and refrigerate.

Preheat the grill to low or wait until the coals are burned down. Pop open a can of beer, take a good swig, and place the can inside the chicken. Position the chicken on the grill so that the chicken sits upright on the grill supported by its legs and the beer can.

Cook over low heat (250°F to 300°F) for at least 2 hours, until golden brown (internal temperature should be 180°F). For the last 15 minutes of cooking, brush the bird with Uncle Sven's. Carve the chickie and serve on Chinette™ paper plates with sides of 5Bs—barbecued baked beans and brown bread. Makes 6 servings.

# Uncle Sven's Secret Sauce

| | |
|---|---|
| 1 cup ketchup | 2 to 3 garlic cloves, minced |
| 1 cup plum jam | Kosher salt and black pepper, freshly |
| ¼ cup Worcestershire sauce | ground |

Mix together all ingredients and season to taste. Makes a generous pint of Uncle Sven's.

---

**THE GODS OF ALL GRILL GODS**

If the beginning of spring heralds the official opening of the "mating season," then let's also declare it a sanctioned "gateway to grilling" national holiday. This holiday is nothing new, however, according to dandy Dionysus and twin bro Bacchus.

These ever-active mythical gods of revelry, refreshment, and ecstatic liberation ingrained in their mortal minds the delights of cooking and "playing" outdoors by throwing a helluva patio party every spring. In fact, the ancient Roman mid-March festival of Bacchanalia was a *compulsory* festival of drunken debauchery, dancing, carousing, and orgies (and to think you were all excited just to break out the new apron and pair of tongs you got for Christmas).

---

# The **S.O.B.**s Are Cookin' Tonight

What's cookin' in those mystical hills of Tennessee? Let's join native son John on a tour to the inner echelon:

> On the first Saturday evening of each month, an assortment of old farmers, and those who wish they had been farmers, gather at an old farmhouse. We have one thing in common—we are the Sons of Belvidere. We tell lies and stories (is there a difference?) and some do things their wives forbid, like smoke cigars and drink a bit (not me).
>
> Several of the bunch pitch in and cook a truly wonderful supper. We eat things our wives would never prepare, like squirrel, rabbit, and fried fish. As one S.O.B. says, "We figure once a month won't kill us." One of the favorite dishes is Falls Mill grits, especially when we have ham. My wife fixes these for me to take—a potful of fresh, stone-ground grits to feed twenty-five or thirty gents. "Them's good eatin!"
>
> Occasionally we feel sorry that our wives miss all this camaraderie and food, so twice a year we invite them for Ladies' Night and cook for them. (They grouse about it, but come anyway.) Before I married, I tried to woo prospective dates with a dish called Chicken Waikiki Beach. . . . The sauce was great.

To make it easy on the poor S.O.B.s on Ladies' Night, I concocted this sure-to-impress recipe, inspired by John's original women-wooing Waikiki chicken. Wild but delightful, the wives will be relieved when it's served . . . right after the possum appetizer.

# Chicken Waikiki Beach Supreme

4 chicken thighs, skinned and boned
4 chicken breasts, skinned and boned

Salt and pepper
1 ripe pineapple, cored and sliced

**Sauce Supreme**
1 cup pineapple juice

1 cup miso
½ cup beer
½ cup soy sauce
½ cup sugar
2 tablespoons sake
4 to 6 garlic cloves, minced
⅓ cup green onions, chopped

Mix up the Sauce Supreme in a large plastic container and marinate the chicken for at least 6 hours, turning the pieces occasionally.

Preheat a gas or charcoal grill to medium-high. Grill the chicken over direct heat, brushing the pieces with additional sauce and turning 2 or 3 times until cooked and tender (about 10 to 12 minutes). Season with salt and pepper if desired.

Right before the chicken is done, brush the pineapple rings with sauce and grill briefly on both sides. Serve the chicken topped with the rings, accompanied by a great salad and some fluffy white rice. Makes 4 to 6 servings.

*Two things are essential in life: to give good dinners
and to keep on fair terms with women.*

—Tallyrand

# Hot Times with the Grateful Gourmet

In an interview years back, when asked how success had changed him (and the Grateful Dead at that time), rhythm guitarist and troubadour Bob Weir philosophized, "I was noticing the other night, for instance, when I'm going through pistachios, opening pistachios . . . the hard-to-open ones? I don't bother with them any more—who's got time?"

Fortunately for fans, "Hot Hand" Bob, who "has a passion for food second only to music," found between tours, time on stage with band Ratdog, and enjoying life with family and friends a nick of time to concoct a line of wickedly wonderful hot sauces sure to jump-start your taste buds. (See page 212 of Red Letter Resources for more information).

Weir, a very strict vegetarian who eats "nothing with a head," shared a favorite recipe for his zesty satay sauce. I added some pistachios and scallops (no head) to the equation and am keeping my fingers crossed it will receive Bobby's blessing. So far, it's batting ten for ten.

## Bob Weir's Peanut Satay Sauce

6 tablespoons Weir's Otherworld Wok
    Sauce or Snake Oil Stir Fry™
6 tablespoons chunky peanut butter

6 tablespoons lite coconut milk
1 teaspoon maple syrup

Combine all ingredients in a bowl. Serve Weir's Peanut Satay Sauce with skewers of headless grilled vegetables (portabello mushrooms, eggplant, baby bok choy . . . ) or some type of grilled meat substitute. Makes approximately 1 cup of satay sauce.

## Pistachio-Crusted Grilled Satay Scallops

1 cup pistachio nutmeats, finely
    ground
16 large sea scallops (about 1½ pounds)

¼ cup Weir's Peanut Satay Sauce
4 large slices fresh pineapple, quartered
4 skewers, soaked in water

Preheat a gas or charcoal grill to medium-high. Cover the surface of a large plate with the ground pistachio nutmeats. Using a pastry brush, "paint" the scallops very lightly with the satay sauce and roll them in the nuts.

Thread four scallops on each of the skewers, securing them at each end with pineapple slices. Grill each side approximately 4 minutes, until the scallops are just cooked through. Serve with a crisp salad. Makes 4 servings.

## "LIFE IS TOO SHORT TO EAT DULL FOOD"

"Alright!" Biker Billy, author of *Biker Billy Cooks with Fire* and *Freeway-a-Fire Cookbook,* is a man's chef who truly loves to play with fire in his kitchen: habanero fire, cayenne fire, jalapeño fire. With zesty recipes like Stuffed Hell's Bells ("Ask not for whom the stuffed bells toll, for they toll for you"), Hot Nutty Noodles (Looking for adventure?), and Billy's rave Murderous Minestrone, you're sure to zap your buds with his off-the-Scoville-charts (zero is mild, 300,000 is atomic) vegetarian cooking.

In fact, Biker Billy, a.k.a. Bill Hufnagle, has been honored by the W. Atlee Burpee™ Seed Company, who named a hot, hybrid jalapeño pepper after him. "I'm the only living person who has a vegetable named after him and his face on a pack of seeds," the Harley-loving fire-eater behind the dark sunglasses recently told me. "It's even better than having a comet named after you—every year I'll be a fire in people's pans, not just a flash in the sky. Eat hot and ride safe!"

*Our first responsibility is to amuse ourselves;*
*if we can't do that, then we can't entertain anyone.*

—Bob Weir

# He Traded His **Shield** for an **Apron**

Since this entire book is about satisfying a man with the meals he loves—a noble mission, no doubt—you won't mind if we toss in a few more quickies to impress the ladies. Let's tell it like it is: The barbecue pit is the coliseum for grill gladiators, an unparalleled arena in which to display tong-wielding wiles, arm muscles flexing as challengers manhandle the meat (and the truth is most women are "grill-submissive"; they prefer the men to take control in the pit).

But if you've taken a time-out and leafed ahead through the next chapter, "How Sweet It Is," you may suddenly be salivating over the prospect of having that Bliss-Out Blackberry Cobbler or Hot Fudge Double Diablo Chocolate Brownie Eskimo Pie™ Sundae being made and served to you.

It is time to plan new seduction strategies: When you invite your darling to dinner, explain how thrilled you are to be grilling dinner for her and how impressed and surprised she'll be with what you're creating (the power of suggestion). Then open your trusty cookbook to the cobbler recipe (page 194) and leave it in plain view next to the chilling bottle of Veuve Clicquot and baskets of fresh blackberries. With the following recipes, you are bound to get . . . um . . . dessert.

# Glazed and Suffused Mighty Macumbo Shrimp

½ cup (1 stick) butter
½ cup honey
1 teaspoon apple cider vinegar
Extra-virgin olive oil
16 colossal prawns (about 1 pound),
  cleaned, shelled, and butterflied

8 ounces Monterey Jack cheese, cut
  into ½-ounce long, thin slices
Salt and pepper
12 to 16 skewers

Preheat a gas or charcoal grill to medium-high. Melt the butter and blend in the honey and vinegar. In a large saucepan, sauté the butterflied prawns in a small amount of olive oil for 2 to 3 minutes, just until they are flexible.

With a pastry brush, paint the shrimp on both sides with the butter-honey mixture. Place the cheese on the "inside" of the shrimp and close, encasing the cheese. Pinch the shrimp around the cheese and thread two skewers through the sides of the shrimp, one at the head and one at the tail, forming an "H" pattern. (You'll be able to fit two to three shrimp on each pair of skewers.)

Grill the shrimp "open" side up, covered, for about a minute, until the cheese begins to melt. Uncover and grill for 3 to 4 minutes more, just until cooked through, brushing with leftover honey-butter. Serve immediately. Makes 6 to 7 appetizers or 3 to 4 entrees.

# *Ahi-Ahi Quickie with Ruby Glaze*

Four 6-ounce ahi tuna steaks
Kosher salt and freshly ground pepper

**Ruby Glaze**
⅓ cup crushed pineapple

⅓ cup brown sugar
⅓ cup water
½ teaspoon ground ginger
1½ cups whole cranberries

---

Prepare the glaze by combining the pineapple, sugar, water, and ginger in a medium saucepan and cooking over medium heat until the sugar is dissolved. Add the cranberries and bring to a boil. Reduce the heat and simmer for 4 to 5 minutes, until the cranberries "pop." Mash the mixture with a fork and remove from heat.

Preheat a gas or charcoal grill to medium-high. Sear the tuna steaks on both sides. Grill for 2 to 3 minutes more on each side (until medium rare), brushing with the Ruby Glaze as the fish cooks; season to taste. Serve tuna with a dollop of glaze on top. Makes 4 servings.

*Most seafoods . . . should be simply threatened*
*with heat and then celebrated with joy.*

—Jeff Smith, *The Frugal Gourmet*

# Fill an Inside Straight with a **S**teak

A game of poker and a steak on the grill— is there a better definition of heaven on earth? Sure . . . add some good bottles of wine and an evening of toasting and bluffing between a group of six friends who have been sharing bonhomie, fine food, and poker tips for more than a decade.

At least with this poker club, if you don't get a good hand, you'll get a hot meal. Card man and chef Don McIlraith lets us in on the game:

> On the first Friday of every month, we get together at a different man's house and the host prepares the dinner. We try to outdo each other with a rotation of theme menus—like meals with as much saturated fat as possible, seasonal meals, meals from around the world. We eat and catch up on each other's lives until it's time to play.
>
> Sometime later, around 11, dessert is served. Favorites include ice cream bonbons, blackberry pie from Toot Sweets with vanilla ice cream (my favorite), ice cream with fresh berries. I am thinking about making a baked Alaska someday, but thinking about it is as close as I have got to serving it.

And what about Don's Poker Club Asian Flank Steak? It's solid; go ahead and bet the pot.

# *P*oker *C*lub *A*sian *F*lank *S*teak

1½ tablespoons fresh ginger root, grated

¼ cup soy sauce

¼ cup Worcestershire sauce

2 tablespoons lemon juice, freshly squeezed

2 teaspoons (2 cloves) garlic, minced

1½-pound flank steak, trimmed

Combine all ingredients, except the steak, in a 9 x 13-inch baking dish. Rinse the steak briefly in cold water and place in the dish, turning over several times to coat with marinade. Cover and refrigerate overnight (turning once or twice).

Preheat a grill to high heat. Grill the flank steak for 4 to 5 minutes per side, until medium rare. Heat the leftover marinade in the microwave or on the grill in a metal pan. Slice the steak diagonally into ¼-inch-thick pieces. Makes 3 to 4 servings.

## HAVE SMOKER, WILL TRAVEL

Try this fantasy on for size; spend an entire summer connecting the dots between barbecue festivals. Mark your travelogue for the best of the best: The Bubba Fest in Spartanburg, South Carolina, where you can enter the Bubba and Bubbette beauty contest; Jack Daniel's™ Invitational in Lynchburg, Tennessee, the top pit stop for barons of barbecue and legends of the coals; Memphis in May, the *Guinness Book of World Records'* largest BBQ competition in the world; and the American Royal in Kansas City, Missouri, America's Superbowl of Barbecue.

# The Art of **Real Barbecuing**

Before you head off for the Bubba Fest, it's essential that you know the difference between grilling and down-home authentic barbecuing. So loosen your belt, get out your pitchforks, and take a journey to the pit with food historian and author Andrew F. Smith. . . .

As a native son of the Golden West, I'm tired of invitations to wimpy "barbecues" in which the host, decked out in an apron and holding a spatula in one hand and a brew in the other, grills meat over charcoal briquettes soaked in lighter fluid. Permit me to offer my never-before-published favorite technique for barbecuing.

| **Ingredients per barrel** | Cheap vinegar or old wine |
|---|---|
| 50-pound chunks of meat (your | (enough to fill up barrel to cover |
| choice of beef or pork) | all ingredients) |
| 2 pounds smashed garlic cloves | Equipment: Backhoe, pitchfork, |
| 2 pounds cut-up onions | wine barrels or deep-wheel barrels, |
| 2 pounds rock salt | mesquite, dried corncobs,matches, |
| 2 pounds jalapeño peppers | deep iron cauldron |

Get your meat 24 hours in advance. Butchering your own cow or pig is best (I prefer the hind end of the cow), but if you have to purchase meat at the butcher, the larger the pieces, the better. Take a washed-off pitchfork and stab the meat several times and stuff the holes with some of the rock salt.

Next, place the chunks of meat in old wine barrels (some men use deep, washed-out wheel barrels). Put the garlic, salt, onions, and peppers into the barrel. Add enough vinegar or old, stale wine to cover the meat. (Whether or not you cover the barrels while the meat marinates generally depends on the quantity of flies and other insects in the neighborhood.) Marinate at least 24 hours.

In the meanwhile, dig with your backhoe a pit about 5 feet deep (the length and width depends upon quantity of meat). Twelve hours before you plan to eat, pile half a pickup load of dried mesquite in the hole. Start a fire, but never use lighter fluid. When the fire is roaring, cover it with a thin layer of dirt and place a layer of corncobs over the dirt.

Using your pitchfork, remove meat from marinade and load the meat in non-flammable gunnysacks. Throw the meat on the corncobs in the hole; cover the meat with another layer of corncobs, then with a layer of dirt.

Cook for about 10 hours, depending on quantity and thickness of meat. Pros can determine readiness by the aroma coming from the pit; some pieces will be blackened, whereas some pieces of meat will be rare—most real men like their meat rare.

While the meat is cooking, remove the marinade from the barrels and ladle it into a cauldron. Position the cauldron over the barbecue pit on an iron rack and let the marinade simmer slowly while the meat is cooking in the pit. This reduced marinade makes a fine sauce. Serves 20 real men or 50 to 75 homeboys.

# You Just Need **Meat** and **Heat**

What do guys love to see on their grills? Steak: T-bone, Porterhouse, filet, rib-eye, flank steaks, sirloins, New York strips, and a great rack of ribs. I could have filled this entire book with ways to heat your meat, but I'm sure you know more about the way you like to grill your goods than I do, so what the hell? In all respect to those of you out there yelling, "Hey! What about Q'd leg of lamb or a damn good pork chop?" Honestly? Other than pinning down the technique of timing, the only other ingredients a respectable Q king needs is meat and heat.

In his book *Bake It Like a Man,* author and meat freak David Bowers holds your hand through a tour of "Meat Street." His golden rules for cooking steak stand firm: Buy the best you can afford; meat must be room temperature; the heat under your grill or pan must be hot, hot, hot; salt and pepper lightly before grilling; and let the meat rest for three minutes after you pull it off the fire so it will be as tender as possible.

Ready? Man your grills. Until I run into grill god Tim O'Neill and beg his legendary Roy's Ribs recipe, we'll have to do with Michael Jordan's favorite steak from his restaurant 23 in Chapel Hill, North Carolina. And you can always go for the all-time over-the-top favorite, steak shish kebobs made by Mom. Hey now!

# Michael Jordan's 23 Delmonico

Four 14-ounce cuts of prime rib-eye
  steak
2 portabella mushrooms
12 sundried tomatoes
Salt and pepper

**Sauce**
¼ cup fresh ginger root, thinly sliced
¼ cup shallots, thinly sliced
¼ cup carrots, thinly sliced
¼ cup celery, thinly sliced
½ cup balsamic vinegar
1 cup reduced veal stock or beef broth
Salt to taste

To prepare the sauce, caramelize the ginger, shallot, carrot, and celery in a large saucepan over medium-high heat. Deglaze pan with balsamic vinegar, reduce by one-half, and add the veal stock or beef broth. Bring to a boil and season to taste.

Preheat a gas or charcoal grill to medium-high. Grill the steak from start to finish, no secrets there! (For a 1½-inch cut, grill for a total of 14 to 16 minutes, depending on how you like your steak done.)

In the meantime, remove stems from the mushrooms and scrape off gills; season and grill until tender. Cut each into triangular segments and alternate on a rosemary skewer: mushroom, sundried tomato, mushroom (three of each). Serve hot with steak.

At Michael Jordan's 23, the Delmonico is served with hot portabella skewers topped with sauce and nestled next to a lavish side of creamy, buttery, Yukon Gold mashed potatoes. Makes 4 servings.

# Mom's Kebobs

1½-pound sirloin steak, cut into 1-inch cubes
2 cups Madge's Own Salad Dressing, divided
15 to 20 colossal stuffed green olives
1 red bell pepper, seeded and cut into large chunks
1 green bell pepper, seeded and cut into large chunks
1 yellow bell pepper, seeded and cut into large chunks
1 large white onion, peeled and cut into quarters
1 pound small mushrooms, scrubbed, stems removed
1 pound new potatoes, parboiled and cut in half
6 skewers

---

In a 9 x 13-inch plastic container, marinate overnight the cubed sirloin in 1 cup of Madge's Own (see page 47) or "any cheap Italian" salad dressing.

One hour before grilling, prepare the vegetables (except the olives) by pouring 1 cup of salad dressing over them, leaving them to marinate before putting them on skewers.

Preheat the grill. Thread the meat, olives, and vegetables onto the skewers in any fashion you desire. Cook over direct medium-high heat, turning often, and baste with extra salad dressing as they cook. Makes 4 servings.

*The best number for a dinner party is two:*
*myself and a damn good head waiter.*

—Nubar Gulbenkian

*Men are hungry. They always have been.*
*They must eat, and when they deny them-*
*selves the pleasures of carrying out that*
*need, they are cutting off part of their*
*fullness, their natural realization of life. . . .*
—M. F. K. Fisher, *The Art of Eating*

# How *Sweet* *It Is*

*Treat Him to His Just Desserts*

HE LOVES . . .

**I**ce cream—I'm addicted to it.—*Richard Gere, actor and activist*

**B**lueberry pie à la mode with bittersweet chocolate ice cream.—*Biker Billy, cookbook author and Harley Man*

**C**hocolate mud cake with an Oreo™ crust served with fresh raspberries and Häagen-Dazs™ vanilla ice cream.—*Potter, Australia*

**N**othing better than a good, gooey, soft chocolate chip cookie with nuts or raisins . . . or a nice rich chocolate mousse with fresh whipped cream. —*Terry, New York*

**M**int chocolate chip ice cream with Hershey's® syrup; when I eat this I feel as close to God as I've ever been. . . .—*Ralph, Nevada*

# The Race Is On

I have discovered that every man has a favorite cookie. It's not a luke-warm "Oh, this is an okay cookie" relationship, but rather a dead-on "If you're going to bake me cookies, don't waste your time on any-thing but *this* cookie" love-is-blind affair. That's why I lost sleep on whether or not I should include the award-winning Margie's Cowboy Cookies™ recipe, the star cookie of my life and bakery.

Over the years, with a tin of Cowboy Cookies in hand, I wheeled and dealed, developed enduring friendships, and won boyfriends. I traded cookies for skis, clothes, backstage concert passes, and hotel accommodations. I loaded the dice at interviews, charmed business associates, and even convinced a car dealer to let me drive away in a new car with no money down and no credit history . . . fun stuff. That's right, with cookies.

The Cowboy Cookies are undeniably the all-time, all-star favorites of most men I know . . . except my man of the moment (who also happens to be my husband). Although I lured him with Cowboy Cookies, he insists now that the only cookies he needs to be happy are my classic chocolate chippers, the power-gems I used to bake for him before ski races (fueling him on, I'm sure, to clinch several na-tional collegiate titles).

As for Margie's Cowboy Cookies? The original, unadulterated recipe is patiently waiting for you in another of my cookbooks, *God-dess in the Kitchen,* along with hundreds of other tried-and-true ways to a man's heart. So get a hold of your copy and go for the gold!

# Champion *C*hip Cookies

½ cup (1 stick) butter, room
   temperature
½ cup (1 stick) margarine, room
   temperature
1 cup brown sugar, unpacked
1 cup white sugar
2 large eggs

1 teaspoon pure vanilla extract
½ teaspoon salt
3 cups unbleached white flour
1 teaspoon baking soda
1 teaspoon baking powder
2½ cups Hershey's® chocolate chips
   (half semi-sweet; half milk chocolate)

---

Preheat the oven to 350°F. In a large mixing bowl, with an electric mixer, beat together the butter, margarine, and sugars until fluffy. Add the eggs, vanilla, and salt and mix well.

Blend together the flour, baking soda, and baking powder, either directly in the measuring cup (my *modus operandi*) or in a large bowl. Tap flour mixture into the creamed mixture and mix on low speed. With a strong wooden spoon, stir in the chocolate chips by hand.

Line a cookie sheet or jellyroll pan (my favorite) with baking parchment and scoop the dough with a 1- to 2-ounce ice cream scoop. Lightly indent the top of the cookie dough mound with a finger.

Bake for 9 to 11 minutes, until the cookies have tiny cracks on top and are golden in color (because ovens vary, note your baking time for the future). Makes about two dozen 2-ounce "Mrs. Fields'™–sized" cookies.

## ALL SEDUCED BY THE FOOD OF THE GODS

It has long been debated why the Swedish botanist Linnaeus came to call chocolate *cacao theobroma*—food of the gods. Some claim it was out of a bold act of gallantry to impress his queen, who was madly addicted to it; others, to his wish to please his confessor. Many simply attribute it to his own ego and passion for chocolate. . . . To each his just desserts.

During the seventeenth century, Catholic clergy in Spain became particularly fond of the new, addictive, sweet sensation that was sweeping the land. Chocoholic Father Escobar even bent the church's rules on fasting with a dose of conveniently twisted spiritual reasoning: he publicly declared (to the profit of his penitents) that ingesting chocolate melted in liquid did not defy strict fasting rules—*Liquidum non frangit jejunium*. And the first cup of hot chocolate was poured.

Centuries later, two obsessed chocolate gods started the Great American Chocolate War. Milton Hershey, a visionary who dreamed of creating a business utopia, and Forrest Mars, the "Howard Hughes of candy," who eventually built a $20-billion-a-year empire, were once partners. When their sweet deal melted, a bitter rivalry arose.

According to the book *Emperors of Chocolate,* "Mars has an extensive intelligence unit . . . to keep a step ahead of its rivals. The company has even recruited the CIA to help it keep abreast of world developments." On the other hand, after Milton made his millions, he promptly gave it all away. Today, Hershey is ministered by a charitable trust that funds one of the wealthiest orphanages in the world. No more mudslinging here—just chocolate.

184

# The Devil Made Me Eat It

President John F. Kennedy was an angel food man through and through, but his late, great brother, Bobby, claimed his favorite dessert was "chocolate cake with chocolate frosting, served with chocolate ice cream and chocolate sauce." Obviously, taste isn't genetic after all.

While I was writing this cookbook, I asked a bunch of men to pick their favorite: "devil's food" or "angel food." Although I was personally shocked at who said what (the guys I would have bet my brownies on to be "devils" turned out to be "angels," and vice versa), the "darker and denser the better" devil-minded men outnumbered the angelically inclined 2 to 1, straight across the board.

The famous designer Halston always played the field and served both at his birthday parties. Some guys wished for a German chocolate choice; others were so stuck in French fantasies of *crème brûlée* and *mousse au chocolat* that they couldn't even choose. So all you horny guys out there, enjoy the ride—until I remount my halo and wings and perfect a recipe for the ultimate angel food cake, we're going to hell in a handbasket of chocolate.

> *I scream, you scream,*
> *We all scream for ice cream. . . .*
> *Tuesdays, Mondays,*
> *We all scream for sundaes. . . .*
> *But, Oh for an Eskimo Pie!*

🍸 185

# Hot Fudge Double *Diablo* Chocolate Brownie Eskimo Pie Sundae

| | |
|---|---|
| **Diablo Hot Fudge** | 3 cups heavy cream, unwhipped |
| 8 ounces unsweetened chocolate | Your favorite brownies |
| 1 pound butter | Your favorite ice cream |
| 7 cups sugar | Whipped cream |

---

In a large heavy-bottomed saucepan over low-low-low-barely any heat (be patient!), melt the chocolate and butter until smooth. Alternately whisk in powdered sugar and cream and stir until shiny and smooth. Leave on low heat for 15 minutes, avoiding boiling at all costs. Stir occasionally.

Prepare—or entice someone else to prepare—your *favorite* recipe for brownies (the Magic Double-Fudge Brownies from *Goddess in the Kitchen* will ensure a delightful sugar coma). Invest in your *favorite* ice cream. Prepare or purchase your *favorite* type of whipped cream.

To assemble the sundae, cut two 3-inch square brownies. Put one brownie in a shallow bowl, top with a scoop of ice cream, and lather with Diablo Hot Fudge. Yes, then repeat the process: brownie, ice cream, hot fudge. Top with real whipped cream and sit back and enjoy the best sugar buzz you'll ever know. Makes approximately 1½ quarts of fudge, which keeps nicely refrigerated and can be reheated in the microwave or in a water bath on the stove whenever you have the urge to indulge.

# The *Sweetest Treats* for the **Birthday Boy**

If you are a wise man, learn to get your birthday cake order in with your favorite baker at least a month ahead of the big day. Regardless of who is the baker, the anticipation of having your cake and eating it too will heighten the taste. Plus, didn't Grandma tell you it is very bad luck to bake your own? My friend Terry Little wistfully wrote, "My mother always made a double- or triple-layer heart-shaped devil's food cake with a creamy, creamy white frosting and red dye in the cake because my birthday is on Valentine's Day." Aw, how sweet . . . I only hope I have the chance to replicate that cake for you someday, Terry.

While hordes of men from the "Food You Love" playground ranted about the joys of carrot cake with cream cheese or butter cream frosting, my hometown friend sent her top-secret recipe (in twenty years she's only shared it with two people) saying, "This marvelous old-fashioned apple cake is my three boys' [one being her hubby] favorite recipe; I bake it for every birthday. Good luck and let me know how it turns out." Thank you, Jan, I feel like I've won the recipe lotto already. And so will all of you when you taste these two jackpots.

> *A good hand for making a sauce is like a good hand*
> *for giving a massage: a valuable and rare attribute.*
>
> —Isabel Allende, *Aphrodite*

☙ 187

# *Miss Jan's Fantasy Apple Cake*

3 cups unbleached white flour

1 teaspoon baking soda

1 teaspoon ground cinnamon

1 teaspoon salt

2 cups sugar

3 large eggs

1¼ cups canola oil

1 teaspoon pure vanilla extract

¼ cup orange juice

2 cups grated apple with peel

1 cup chopped walnuts

1 cup angel flake coconut

**Buttermilk Dream Sauce**

½ cup buttermilk

½ cup butter

1 cup sugar

½ teaspoon baking soda

Preheat the oven to 325°F. Sift together the flour, baking soda, cinnamon, and salt and set aside. In a large mixing bowl, combine the sugar, eggs, oil, vanilla, and orange juice. Beat until well blended. Stir in the flour mixture. When all ingredients are well mixed, fold in the apple, nuts, and coconut. Spoon the batter into a well-greased and floured 10 x 4-inch angel cake tube pan. Bake for 90 minutes.

Begin mixing the buttermilk sauce as soon as the cake is in the oven. In a large heavy-bottomed saucepan, combine the buttermilk, butter, and sugar and heat over medium heat, stirring constantly, until the mixture boils. Add the baking soda and stir like crazy (the sauce goes wild; take care to avoid overflow). Turn off the heat and allow the buttermilk sauce to sit while the cake bakes.

When the cake is done, remove it from the oven and allow it to cool in the pan for 15 minutes. While the cake is cooling, reheat the buttermilk sauce on a low, low setting.

Turn the cooled cake out onto a serving plate. Puncture the cake deeply, top to bottom and all over—go for it—with an ice pick or similar utensil; it's the secret to getting the cake to absorb the sauce.

With a pastry brush or spatula, "paint" the entire surface of the cake until the sauce is gone, allowing the cake to fully absorb the sauce. Let it stand at least 1 hour before cutting. Makes 8 to 12 servings, depending on the size of the birthday boy and his friends.

### THE INSIDE LINE

The birthday cake goddess adds, "What I have learned after baking this cake over the last twenty years is it truly must be baked the day before you need it; it is wonderfully moist on the second and subsequent days. Also, I use powdered buttermilk just because it is so convenient; just stir the powdered buttermilk into the sugar ahead before heating with the butter to avoid lumps." Smooth operating.

> *So are you to my thoughts as food to life,*
> *Or as sweet-season'd showers are to the ground.*

—Shakespeare, *Sonnet LXXV*

# Blind Date Carrot Cake with Butter Cream Frosting

| | |
|---|---|
| 1 cup sugar | 2 cups unbleached flour |
| 4 eggs, room temperature | ½ cup buttermilk |
| 2 teaspoons pure vanilla extract | 4 cups peeled and finely grated carrots |
| 1 cup canola oil | 1 cup crushed pineapple, drained |
| 1 teaspoon salt | 1½ cups medjool dates, pitted and |
| 1 tablespoon ground cinnamon | finely chopped |
| 1 teaspoon ground allspice | 1½ cup pecans, chopped |
| 2 teaspoons baking soda | ½ cup angel flake coconut (optional) |

Preheat oven to 350°F. Grease one 9 x 13-inch or two 9-inch round baking pans.

In a large mixing bowl, beat together the sugar, eggs, vanilla, oil, salt, and spices. Blend the soda into the flour and then alternately mix in gently the flour and buttermilk. Fold in carrots, pineapple, dates, pecans, and coconut, if you wish.

Pour the batter into prepared pan(s) and bake for 20 to 25 minutes, until a toothpick comes out clean or the cake springs back when pressed with your finger. When completely cooled, frost with a butter cream or cream cheese frosting.

# ℬutter **C**ream **F**rosting

½ cup (1 stick) sweet butter, softened
3½ cups (1 pound) powdered sugar
¾ teaspoon pure vanilla extract

¼ teaspoon lemon juice
5 tablespoons half-and-half

---

With an electric mixer on low speed, cream the butter, sugar, vanilla, and lemon juice. Slowly add the half-and-half until the frosting is creamy. Beat well, but do not overmix or the frosting will separate. Ice up! Will frost one 9-inch two-layer cake, a 9 x 13-inch cake, or one dozen cupcakes.

> *Ideally, the body of a woman should feel*
> *like a hot water bottle filled with Devonshire cream.*
>
> —Kurt Vonnegut

🍸 191

## KITCHEN QUARTERBACKING 101

To avoid technical blunders in the kitchen, particularly when baking, memorize this checklist:

- Always use an audible timer.

- Know your oven; check for its "real" temperature with an oven thermometer.

- Set your timer a few minutes before the recipe's "done" time. To check if done, use your senses (sight, smell, touch, intuition), the toothpick test (insert; it should come out clean), or the touch test (should spring back when touched).

- Can you say "Baker's Joy™"? This is, hands down, the best item on the market for greasing and flouring your pans.

- Use baking parchment paper to line sheet pans (bribe the counter person at your local bakery).

- Avoid extremes. Unless specified otherwise, work with room temperature ingredients.

- Open and shut the oven door in slow motion.

# Cobbler of the **G**ods

There's more than just cobbler cooking at Cynthia's Restaurant in Los Angeles, but it's owner Cynthia Hirsh's blackberry cobbler that has been responsible for triggering divine revelations among the stars and others: "This is God," declared a smitten Steve Martin after dishing into the cobbler. Word is that superstar Tom Cruise has been known to cruise Cynthia's to indulge in his favorite temptation, the same sinfully celestial cobbler of the gods.

Further north at Lark Creek Inn in Larkspur, California, guys are starry-eyed over chef Bradley Ogden's favorite, his Nectarine Blueberry Crisp. After begging Chef Ogden for his coveted, top-secret man-pleaser—the Butterscotch Pudding—to no fruition, so to speak, I finally settled for this heavenly crisp after testing it out on some very happy men. Inspired by Cynthia's blackberry cobbler and the King of Cobbler recipe from cobbler god Michael Pontecorvo, I proudly offer you my version of palatal ecstasy.

*Wheresoever she was, there was Eden.*

—Mark Twain

# Bliss-Out Blackberry Cobbler

2 pints fresh blackberries
¼ cup light brown sugar
1½ teaspoons cornstarch

**Topping**
½ cup brown sugar

2 tablespoons instant oatmeal
2 tablespoons flour
2 tablespoons unsalted butter, softened
Pinch nutmeg

Preheat the oven to 375°F. In a medium bowl, gently combine the blackberries, brown sugar, and cornstarch. In another bowl, combine all the topping ingredients with a fork until crumbly.

Spoon the berry mixture into an 8-inch square baking dish or four individual ramekins and sprinkle the topping over the berries. Bake for 35 to 40 minutes, until it is hot and bubbly. Serve warm, topped with vanilla Häagen-Dazs™ ice cream and bliss out! Makes 4 servings.

# Bradley Ogden's Nectarine Blueberry Crisp

**Topping**
¾ cup flour
⅓ cup light brown sugar, packed
⅓ cup white sugar

¼ teaspoon salt
¼ teaspoon ground cinnamon
⅛ teaspoon ground ginger
6 tablespoons cold unsalted butter

**Fruit Filling**
1½ pounds firm, ripe nectarines,
  pitted and sliced ½-inch thick

1 pint fresh blueberries
¼ cup sugar
2 tablespoons flour

---

Preheat the oven to 400°F. In a medium bowl, prepare the topping by mixing together the flour, sugars, salt, and spices. Cut in the butter until the mixture resembles coarse meal.

Prepare the fruit filling by tossing together the pitted and sliced nectarines, blueberries, sugar, and flour. Pour the fruit mixture into a 9- or 10-inch square baking dish. Sprinkle the topping evenly over the fruit.

Bake for 25 to 30 minutes, until the top is browned and the juices are bubbling up around the edges. Cool for 15 minutes before serving topped with ice cream or whipped cream. Makes 6 servings.

---

**SHE'S A REAL DISH**

Feeling like a half-baked Napoleon who needs a new cupcake in your life? Set your taste buds up on a blind date with one of these sweeties:

| | | |
|---|---|---|
| Crème Yvette | Brown Betty | Sara Lee |
| Charlotte | Charlotte Martinique | Madeleine |
| Sally Lunn | Lady Baltimore | Margarita |
| Sherry | Peach Melba | Zara |

# Doing the **San Francisco Tarantella**

Call it research. For one college social-psych class, I risked my grade to conduct a little experiment on my classmates by blindfolding everyone and giving them a plate of tiramisu. Not quite like the acid tests back in the colleges of the '60s, but still. . . . Hoping to determine different levels of conditioned perception, I asked them all to name what they were experiencing, while I took notes and asked questions. After the teacher had his, I got an easy A.

May I present to you, the Chocolate Passion Childhood Java Pudding Cream Dream Chocolate Celebration Chilled Wicked Wonder Chocolate-Almond Spunelli Chilled Mocha Java Passionate Pudding Chocolate Tarantella Creamy Java Cake.

This recipe, from someone who really knows her tiramisu, is mondo rich, utterly divine, and simple. GraceAnn Walden, a restaurant columnist for the *San Francisco Chronicle,* conducts history-food-walking tours of the Golden Gate City's traditional Italian neighborhood North Beach (see Red Letter Resources on page 211 for more information) and keeps her Italian American boyfriend, Ray, in a tiramisu state of mind claiming, "It's great to snack on in bed." *Che buono!*

> *Good company, good wine, good welcome*
> *Can make good people.*
>
> —Shakespeare, *Henry VIII*

# $\mathcal{T}$*iramisu*

One 8-ounce tub mascarpone cheese
1 large egg, beaten
1 cup heavy cream
½ cup sugar
1 teaspoon vanilla
½ cup espresso or dark roast coffee

2 shots (about 6 tablespoons) rum or
  brandy
Two 6-ounce packages soft ladyfingers
  (prefer Lazzaroni™)
One 2-ounce chunk dark chocolate

---

In a large bowl, whip the mascarpone and the beaten egg with an electric hand mixer until fluffy and set aside.

In another bowl, whip together the cream, sugar, and vanilla until gently incorporated into a nice soft texture, but not too stiff (soft-peak stage). Fold the whipped cream mixture into the mascarpone-egg mixture and set aside (keep chilled). Mix the liquor with the coffee and set aside.

Arrange the ladyfingers in an 8 x 8-inch square baking dish or a spring form pan lined with wax paper, cutting them to form a "tight" fit over the entire surface of the dish.

Assemble the cake by sprinkling one-half of the spiked coffee mixture evenly over the ladyfingers. Top this with at least an inch of the mascarpone cream mixture and a dusting of grated chocolate.

Repeat the layer: ladyfingers, spiked coffee, mascarpone cream. Blanket the top of the tiramisu with a generous amount of grated chocolate. Cover with aluminum foil and refrigerate at least 5 hours before serving. Makes 8 to 12 servings.

# ℳascarpone in a Pinch

¾ pound cream cheese
¼ pound ricotta
2 tablespoons whipping cream

1 tablespoon fresh lemon juice
1 tablespoon sugar

---

Combine ingredients and beat or process until creamy and smooth. Will keep refrigerated for up to a week. Makes 1 pound.

*I raised to my lips a spoonful of the cake. . . .*
*A shudder ran through my whole body*
*and I stopped, intent upon the extraordinary changes*
*that were taking place.*

—Marcel Proust, *Remembrance of Things Past*

# Try a Slice of **Immortality**

A friend recently told me she had gone to dinner with a group of friends, eight men being among them, and when it was time for dessert, every single man ordered cheesecake. Need I say more?

What is the cheesecake of men's dreams? Some swear by Lindy's. Other's bet on Junior's. One common denominator is the name must be preceded with two magic words, *New York:* New York cheesecake. (I've always wondered how "Philadelphia" brand cream cheese fits into the equation.)

Men have called my cheesecake by many names when they were begging me to make it. Some of the craftiest call-names include the "Jesus Cheesecake" ("Jesus, this is good!"), "Indy Cheesecake" ("Yours does the Indy around Lindy's!"), and the "Weekly Cheese-cake" (serves one man for a week).

I have always called my masterpiece "Casablanca" simply because I have no doubt that if Ilsa had baked up a cake for Rick, he would have *never* let her get on that plane so many rainy nights ago—and never, *ever* without leaving him the recipe. You can sometimes change fate and uncross the stars as easy as baking something a man loves.

# Casablanca Cheesecake

From *Goddess in the Kitchen*

**Crust**

2½ cups Petit Buerre™ wafers or
   graham crackers, crushed
5 tablespoons melted butter
¼ cup sugar
½ teaspoon nutmeg

**Topping**

1½ cups sour cream
3 tablespoons sugar
½ teaspoon vanilla
Pinch of salt
Fresh fruit for garnish (optional)

**Filling**

2½ pounds cream cheese (the real
   stuff; no substitutes), room
   temperature
1¾ cups sugar
1 teaspoon pure vanilla extract
1½ teaspoons lemon zest, freshly
   grated
¼ teaspoon salt
3 tablespoons flour
5 whole eggs plus 2 egg yolks,
   room temperature
½ cup heavy cream

To prepare the crust, combine all ingredients in a small bowl with a fork. Line a 10-inch springform pan with baking parchment and press the crust mixture onto the bottom and partially up the sides of the pan with the flat bottom of a glass or measuring cup. Chill while preparing filling.

Preheat oven to 400°F. To make the filling, beat the cream cheese until fluffy in a large mixing bowl. Add the sugar, vanilla, lemon zest, salt, and flour and beat well. Add the eggs and yolks, *one at a time,* beating or whisking after each egg. Gently blend in the heavy cream. Pour the filling into the prepared pan and bake for 7 minutes; reduce heat to 225°F and bake for an additional 70 to 80 minutes.

While the cheesecake is baking, form the topping by whisking together all of the ingredients in a small bowl. Without removing it from the oven, gently spread the topping over the cheesecake (take care not to "jiggle" it too much). Increase oven temperature to 400°F and bake for another 5 to 7 minutes.

Cool at room temperature and refrigerate at least 2 hours before serving. A fresh fruit garnish always adds a classic touch. Makes 10 to 12 servings or serves one man for a week.

*There is no end.*
*There is no beginning.*
*There is only the infinite passion of life.*

—Federico Fellini

## And the Winner Is . . . Your **American Pie**

Some say it's the texture, some say it's the taste. Some say it's the memory of the front porch swing or the dinner table of childhood where you felt utterly princely when Mom would deliver that favorite slice of pie à la mode with the sweetest smile on her face. Some don't even know why, but if you ask any man "What is the quintessential American pie?" he'll tell you.

In the movie *Reindeer Games*, Ben Affleck's Rudy had his palate primed for pecan pie all the way from his prison cell. It's also no surprise that the all-American apple pie rides high on the pieway to heaven. What is revealing is how other fruity or creamy favorites— rhubarb, cherry, blueberry, banana cream, pumpkin—are mentioned more often and more *passionately* than most. The debate is sure to rage.

The other two queens of the American pie prom, according to masses of males, are the soulful, aphrodisiacal sweet potato pie and the luscious lemon meringue (my dad's favorite). In the meanwhile, feast on these and send in your ballot.

# **S**weet **P**otato *A*merican **P**ie

3 pounds (3 to 4) Louisiana yams
1 unbaked deep-dish 9-inch pie shell
   (see page 208 for recipe)
½ cup white sugar
½ cup brown sugar
6 tablespoons butter, melted
1 teaspoons ground cinnamon
¾ teaspoon ground nutmeg

½ teaspoon ground ginger
¼ teaspoon salt
3 eggs, well beaten
½ cup evaporated milk
¼ cup orange juice, freshly squeezed
2 tablespoons bourbon whiskey
1 tablespoon orange zest

---

Peel the yams, cut them into large cubes, and boil in water over medium heat until tender and mashable, about 25 minutes. Meanwhile, prepare the pie crust. Refrigerate the shell until ready to use. When the yams are done, mash them well (yields about 2½ cups mashed yams).

Preheat the oven to 400°F. In a large bowl, mix the hot mashed yams with the sugars, butter, spices, and salt and beat until light and smooth. Add the beaten eggs and mix well. Finally, add the milk, orange juice, bourbon, and orange zest and blend until creamy.

Pour the mixture into the unbaked pie shell. Put the pie in the oven and immediately turn the temperature down to 350°F. Bake for 45 to 55 minutes or until the center of the pie is set (a knife inserted will come out clean). Makes 8 servings.

# Lemon *Heaven* Meringue Pie

One prebaked 9-inch pie shell
  (see page 208 for recipe)

3 tablespoons butter
2 teaspoons lemon zest

**Lemon Heaven Filling**
5 large egg yolks, room temperature,
  lightly beaten
1 cup sugar
⅓ cup cornstarch
1½ cups water
½ cup lemon juice, freshly squeezed
  with pulp (3 to 4 lemons)

**In the Clouds Meringue**
5 eggs whites
⅛ teaspoon cream of tartar
Pinch of salt
½ cup sugar

---

Make the dough and bake the crust (see The Inside Line on page 206).

Separate the eggs, placing the whites in a grease-free, straight-sided glass bowl. Grate the zest from the lemons, then squeeze the juice from the lemons; remove seeds (Meyer lemons are the best).

Without heat, combine the sugar and cornstarch in a medium heavy-bottomed saucepan. Add the water, stirring until smooth. Add the egg yolks and stir until velvety.

Place the pan over medium-low heat and bring contents to a slow boil, stirring constantly (do not walk away!). Once the mixture comes to a boil, boil for 1 minute. Remove from heat and stir in the lemon juice, butter, and lemon zest. Set aside to cool.

Preheat the oven to 400°F. To make the meringue, add the cream of tartar and salt to the egg whites and beat with an electric mixer at medium speed until foamy. Gradually add the sugar and continue beating on high speed until stiff peaks form.

Spoon the cooled lemon filling into the prebaked pie shell, smoothing the top with the back of a spoon. With a large, clean spoon, spread a ½-inch flat layer of meringue over the filling and onto the edge of the crust (to "seal" and prevent shrinking). Then spoon the rest of the meringue on top of the pie, shaping it into dramatically high peaks with the back of the spoon.

Bake the pie in the center of the oven for 6 to 8 minutes or until the meringue is golden and the tips are flecked with brown. Cool the pie on a wire rack. Transports 8 to taste-bud heaven.

> *Aphrodisiacs are the bridge*
> *between gluttony and lust.*
>
> —Isabel Allende

**THE INSIDE LINE**

Ah, prebaking a pie shell. Don't balk; do it once and you'll have it wired. Make the pie dough first (or just buy one). If you make it, conserve your time and energy and always make a double-crust recipe, even if you're only using one dough ball (the dough freezes perfectly for up to a couple of weeks if well wrapped).

Using a glass or ceramic pie plate, flute the edges of the crust extra-high because it will "slink" down when baking. Refrigerate dough for 15 to 20 minutes before baking.

Preheat the oven to 400°F. Prick bottom of crust several times with a fork. Place baking parchment over the dough and line with weights, a stainless steel pie "chain" (my favorite), uncooked macaroni, or beans.

Bake for 7 minutes, remove weighting material and parchment, and bake 2 more minutes until golden. Cool before filling. Or you can forgo the damn weights and extra hassle, prick the bottom, and just cook the crust *au naturel* for 7 to 9 minutes, letting the sides slink down as they may.

*Eat, friends, drink,*
*and be drunk with love.*

—Song of Solomon 5:1

# The Sure-Fire Way
# to Keep His **"Heart On"**

Clams, oysters, mushrooms, bananas, apples, artichokes, seafood, tomatoes, parsley, chili powder, nutmeg, cinnamon, asparagus, truffles, chocolate, champagne, *the imagination* . . . the list of aphrodisiacs is as endless as the brain waves of a man thinking about sex.

Every man I ever cooked for, and I mean *really* cooked for, is still intrigued to this day by the aphrodisiacal powers they think I sprinkled in their food. They all fell under the spell of my "Fab Four": I caught them with Cowboy Cookies (story on page 182), teased them with Love Apple Linguine (see page 81), sustained them with the Magnificent Meatloaf (on page 142), and then lit their fire with my apple pie.

I offer you now the most powerful aphrodisiac that has ever graced my kitchen. If the truth be known, it was not an apple with which Eve tempted Adam on that fateful day in Paradise, but rather a hot, bubbling, succulent, homemade apple pie. If an apple a day keeps the doctor away, with this recipe and a sexy lover to spoon-feed it to you, you won't need a prescription for Viagra® anymore. C'mon, just take one bite, baby. . . .

# Apple *Piagra*

**Double-Crust Perfect Pie Dough**

2 cups unbleached flour

1¼ teaspoons salt

¼ teaspoon baking powder

½ cup *cold* Crisco™ shortening

⅓ cup *cold* margarine or butter

⅓ cup *ice* water

**Topping**

¼ cup flour

¼ cup "sugar in the raw"

1 teaspoon cinnamon

3 tablespoons chilled butter

**Filling**

7 to 8 McIntosh or Golden Delicious
   apples

3 tablespoons DeKuyper® Sour Apple
   Pucker™ Schnapps

⅔ cup "sugar in the raw"

2 tablespoons flour

2 teaspoons cinnamon

1 teaspoon nutmeg

1 teaspoon pure vanilla

1 teaspoon lemon juice

Pinch of salt

---

Make the dough first. Blend together the dry ingredients. Cut in the shortening and margarine or butter with a fork or pastry cutter until you achieve a fine, crumbly texture. Dribble cold water over the flour mixture and mix together. Form 2 dough balls. Using sweeping strokes from the center of the dough toward the outer edge, on a well-floured, cool surface, roll one ball to a ⅛-inch thickness. Line a 10-inch deep-dish glass or ceramic pie plate with the dough.

Peel, core, and slice apples. (An apple peeler, like the one available from L. L. Bean™, makes this task quick and simple.) Put them in a large bowl.

Sprinkle Sour Apple Pucker over the apples and set aside for a few minutes to let the schnapps do its magic. Then toss together the apples, sugar, flour, spices, vanilla, lemon juice, and salt. Line the pie shell with the apple mixture and gently press into shape.

To make the topping, mix together the flour, sugar, and cinnamon in a small bowl. Using a fork, cut the chilled butter into the flour mixture until it takes on a crumbly texture. Sprinkle it on top of the apples.

Preheat the oven to 400°F. Roll out the second ball of dough and place it on top of your pie, using dabs of cold water to adhere the top crust to the bottom crust. Cut several small slits on the top crust for steam to escape. Cut off excess dough, leaving 1 inch of dough to turn under and flute.

With the leftover pie dough, roll out and cut out letters for the lucky man's name, the letters "I♥U," or any other special fertility symbol you may have in mind. Seal these symbols to the top of the pie using a touch of water. Sprinkle a little raw sugar on top.

Bake at 400°F for 10 minutes. Reduce the heat to 350°F and bake for 50 more minutes, until the Piagra is a tempting golden-brown color. Serve with a scoop of favorite ice cream. Makes 1 dose of Piagra; cures 1 to 8 men.

*They eat, they drink, and in communion sweet*
*Quaffing immortality and joy.*

—John Milton

# Red Letter Resources

## Endzones for Epicures

**Dean & Deluca**
Locations throughout the United States
Phone: 800 221-7714
Web: *www.deandeluca.com*
*A chef's fantasy store, catalog, and specialty foods*

**Falls Mill and Country Store**
134 Falls Mill Road
Belvidere, TN 37306
Phone: 931 469-7161
Web: *www.fallsmill.com*
*Water-powered stone-ground grits, cornmeal, flour, multigrain pancake mix, and cookbook*

**GraceAnn Walden**
*San Francisco Chronicle* restaurant columnist
Web: *www.koit.com/koit/food.cfm#*
E-mail: yummy@sirius.com
*Food-history-walking tours of San Francisco's Italian North Beach*

**King Arthur Flour Company**
P. O. Box 876
Norwich, VT 05055-0876
Phone: 800 827-6836
Web: *www.KingArthurFlour.com*
*The* Baker's Catalogue *features "must haves" like SAF-Instant™ yeast*

**Kitchen D'Orr Spices**
Blended by Chef Daniel Orr of Guastavino's
Phone: 800 835-7603
*www.kitchendorr.com*
*www.flavorbank.com*

**Sur La Table**
1765 Sixth Avenue South
Seattle, WA 98134
Phone: 800 243-0852
*www.surlatable.com*
Locations throughout the United States
*Specialty foods, kitchen gear, and more*

**Weir's Sauces**
773 Magellan Way
Napa, CA 94559
Phone: 415 884-5849
Web: *www.weirsauces.com*
E-mail: weirsauces@dead.net
*Hot sauces and cooking oils*
*All net profits from the sales of Weir's Sauces*
*go to the Furthur Foundation, which*

*supports environmental, children's*
*education, and homeless causes.*

**Williams-Sonoma**
Locations throughout the United States
Phone: 800 541-2233
Web: *www.williamssonoma.com*
*Specialty foods, kitchen gear, culinary*
*wonders*

## Tasty Pages for Men Who Love Food

*The Art of Eating*
by M. F. K. Fisher

*Bake It Like a Man: A Real Man's Cookbook*
by David Bowers and Sharon Bowers

*The Best of Craig Claiborne: More Than*
*1,000 Recipes from His Cooking Columns*
*in the New York Times*
by Craig Claiborne with Pierre Franey

*Biker Billy Cooks with Fire: Robust Recipes*
*from America's Most Outrageous Televi-*
*sion Chef and Biker Billy's Freeway-a-Fire*
*Cookbook: Life's Too Short to Eat Dull*
*Food*

by Bill Hufnagle (Fire up with Biker Billy
at *www.bikerbilly.com*)

*Bobby Flay's Boy Meets Grill*
by Bobby Flay and Joan Schwartz

*Bradley Ogden's Breakfast, Lunch,*
*and Dinner*
by Bradley Ogden

*Cajun Men Cook: Recipes, Stories and*
*Food Experiences from Louisiana*
*Cajun Country*
by the Beaver Club of Lafayette

*Chef Paul Prudhomme's Louisiana Tastes: Exciting Flavors from the State That Cooks* by Paul Prudhomme

*Cooking Healthy with a Man in Mind: A Healthy Exchanges Cookbook* by Joanna M. Lund with Barbara Alpert

*Curtis Cooks with Heart and Soul: Quick, Healthy Cooking from the Host of TV's "From My Garden"* by Curtis G. Aikens

*The Daniel Boulud's Café Boulud Cookbook: French-American Recipes for the Home Cook* by Daniel Boulud and Dorie Greenspan

*Daniel Orr Real Food: Smart and Simple Meals and Menus for Entertaining* by Daniel Orr

*Dude Food: Recipes for the Modern Guy* by Karen Brooks, Gideon Bosker, and Reed Darmon

*Eat Dangerously Cookbook* by Benjamin Lewis and Rodrigo Paranhos Velloso (Satisfy your inner hedonist at *www.eatdangerously.com*)

*Every Day's a Party: Louisiana Recipes for Celebrating with Family and Friends* by Emeril Lagasse

*Goddess in the Kitchen: 201 Heavenly Recipes, Spirited Stories and Saucy Secrets* by Margie Lapanja

*A Guy's Guide to Great Eating: Big-Flavored Fat-Reduced Recipes for Men Who Love to Eat* by Don Mauer

*How to Eat: The Pleasures and Principles of Good Food* by Nigella Lawson

*Jacques Pepin's Table: The Complete Today's Gourmet* by Jacques Pepin

*LaBelle Cuisine: Recipes to Sing About* by Patti LaBelle with Laura B. Randolph

*A Man and His Pan* by John Boswell with Susan Wyler

*The Man Who Ate Everything* by Jeffrey Steingarten

*Mario Batali Holiday Food: Family Recipes for the Most Festive Time of Year*
by Mario Batali

*The Men of the Pacific Street Social Club Cook: Homestyle Recipes and Unforgettable Stories*
by Gerard Renny

*Newman's Own Cookbook*
by Paul Newman and A. E. Hotchner

*The Oxford Companion to Food*
by Alan Davidson

*Simple Italian Food: Recipes from My Two Villages*
by Mario Batali

*Taste: One Palate's Journey through the World's Greatest Dishes*
by David Rosengarten

*Weber's Art of the Grill: Recipes for Outdoor Living*
by Weber-Stephen Products Company and Jamie Purviance (Do the "Q" at *www.weberbbq.com*)

# Hot Links for Web-Wielding Guys and Gourmands

*www.aeb.org*
The American Egg Board official site; recipes and more

*www.barbecuen.com*
Barbecue recipes, links, facts, forums, restaurants, and online store

*www.bigspud.com*
The potato recipe collection

*www.charlietrotters.com*
Recipes, information, and newsletter

*www.chefscatalog.com*
Professional restaurant equipment for the home chef

*www.chefsecret.net*
Culinary resource site with food links staffed by professional chefs

*www.crateandbarrel.com*
Home and kitchen wares, specialty foods, and more

*www.cuisinenet.com*
Online restaurant guide

*www.culinarycafe.com*
Food, recipes, and resources

*www.epicurious.com*
Food and drink recipes and archives,
  *Bon Appetit* and *Gourmet* magazine
  home pages, resources, cookbook
  reviews, shopping, and more

*www.foodandwine.com*
Magazine highlights and extensive recipe
  archive

*www.foodtv.com*
Television Food Network's gateway to
  recipes, entertaining, celebrity chefs,
  and television cooking shows

*www.greatfood.com*
An online gourmet food store

*www.grits.com*
Keep your special Bubba happy with grits

*www.ichef.com*
Internet chef online magazine

*www.maravonda.com*
Premium mail-order coffee merchant

*www.menstuff.org*
Lifestyle resources, cookbooks, forums,
  and more

*www.ribman.com*
Ribs, ribs, and more ribs; recipes, links,
  and restaurant locator

*www.sallys-place.com*
Award-winning culinary site, international
  food scene, and articles

*www.slowfood.com*
The official page of the International Slow
  Food Movement

*www.starchefs.com*
Recipes from chefs and cookbook authors

*www.tavolo.com*
Specialty foods, kitchenware, recipes, and
  shopping

*www.tomlagana.com*
Newsletter, nutrition, and "Chicken
  Soup" inspiration

*www.westpointmarket.com*
Upscale specialty food shop

# Acknowledgments

- First and foremost, I am most grateful to everyone who "played" by entrusting me with their recipes, insights, stories, and deep personal secrets ("Devil's food or angel food, guys?"), freely giving their time and culinary gifts to make this collection of love potions come alive. Blessings to all—thank you so much!

- To Vojko, because you are who you are—shine on!

- To Lila Grace, always and forever my best friend.

- To Brenda Knight, for holding my space on the playground when I needed a minute to refocus on all the hungry men after playing with the frisky goddesses.

- To my dazzling duo of editors, Leslie Berriman and Heather McArthur, for paving these pages with the style and grace of your lively pens; to Leah Russell, my publicity goddess; and to everyone at Conari Press who put their magic touch on this book—three's a charm!

- To Michael J. Beiser, for blessing and energizing my life (and my manuscript).

- To Shivani, with love, for sharing your secrets of "sensuous success"—I am loving my dreams to life, inspired by you.

- To Kimberly Terrell, for your incomparably original and hilarious brain waves and words; I owe you a few.

- To Chyrise Broyer, for your faith and friendship and for helping me manifest Jupiter.

- To all the messengers—Laurie Woolever, Irma Brandt, John Heisler, Dennis McNally, Kim Thomas, Carol Henry, Lissa Ciccio-Velez, Paula Davis, Peter Grills, and Kathy Hatch for your generous assistance.

- To my muses and mentors—Denyse Hughes, Dragica Lapanja, Dorismarie Welcher, Kelly Douglass, Cassidy Law Sears, Ambrosia Healy, Linda Azar, Grace Fuller, Linda D. Graber, Kate Towle, Cindy Coverdale, Kristina Hill, Bob and Chris Blanchard, Kathryn Grenda, Paula Wilson, Jocelyn Brumbaugh, Mary Heintz, Paul Hughes, Peter Quah Perkins, The O'Neill Clan, Skip Bertuzzi, Wayne Pate, Terry Little, Joe Beiser, Notre Dame, and the Holy Spirit for your presence in my life.

# Works Cited

Allende, Isabel. *Aphrodite: A Memoir of the Senses*. New York: Harper-Collins, 1998.

Batali, Mario. *Mario Batali Simple Italian Food: Recipes from My Two Villages*. New York: Clarkson Potter, 1998.

Bowers, David, and Sharon Bowers. *Bake It Like a Man: A Real Man's Cookbook*. New York: William Morrow and Company, Inc., 1999.

Brenner, Joel Glenn. *The Emperors of Chocolate*. New York: Random House, 1999.

California's Contra Costa County Cowbelles. *Culinary Collaborations*. Copyright pending: 1980.

Cunningham, Marion. *The Breakfast Book*. New York: Alfred A. Knopf, Inc., 1987.

De Sola, Ralph, and Dorothy De Sola. *A Dictionary of Cooking*. New York: Meredith Press, 1969.

Farb, Peter, and George Armelagos. *Consuming Passions: The Anthropology of Eating*. Boston: Houghton Mifflin Company, 1980.

Fisher, M. F. K. *The Art of Eating*. New York: Vintage Books, 1976.

Flay, Bobby, and Joan Schwartz. *Boy Meets Grill*. New York: Clarkson Potter, 1999.

Foxworth, Jo. *The Bordello Cookbook*. Wakefield, R.I.: Moyer Bell, 1997.

Ginsberg, Merle. "High Gere." *W,* August 1999.

Herbst, Sharon Tyler. *Never Eat More Than You Can Lift and Other Food Quotes and Quips*. New York: Broadway Books, 1997.

Jacobs, Jay. *The Eaten Word*. New York: Birch Lane Press, 1995.

LaBelle, Patti. *LaBelle Cuisine*. New York: Broadway Books, 1999.

Lagasse, Emeril. *Every Day's a Party*. New York: William Morrow and Company, Inc., 1999.

Lorwin, Madge. *Dining with William Shakespeare*. New York: Atheneum, 1976.

Maloberti, Elisa. "Re: Food Men Love." Personal e-mail, 7 February 2000.

Riches, Derrick. "Barbecues and Grilling." *About*. telnet:// bbq.about.com/index.htm (15 April 2000).

Schivelbusch, Wolfgang. *Tastes of Paradise: A Social History of Spices, Stimulants, and Intoxicants*. New York: Vintage Books, 1992.

Simon, David R. "Re: Food Men Love." Personal e-mail, 26 February 2000.

Singer, Natasha. "SWM, Slightly Fragrant, Looking for SWF Handy with an Ax." *Gentlemen's Quarterly,* April 2000.

Smith, Andrew F. *Pure Ketchup: A History of America's National Condiment*. Charlestown: University of South Carolina Press, 1996.

Villas, James. *James Villas' The Town and Country Cookbook*. Boston: Little, Brown, and Company, 1985.

The Wild Women Association. *Wild Women in the Kitchen: 101 Rambunctious Recipes and 99 Tasty Tales.* Berkeley, Calif.: Conari Press, 1996.

Young, Bob, and Al Stankus. *Jazz Cooks: Portraits and Recipes of the Greats.* New York: Stewart, Tabori & Chang, 1992.

# Index

Affleck, Ben, 202
Ahi-Ahi Quickie with Ruby Glaze, 172
angel food cake, 185
aphrodisiacs, 2, 6, 9, 114, 127, 170, 207
Aphrodite, 9, 113–14, 127
Appetizers
  Cadillac Ranch Dip, 96
  Ceviche Ecuatoriano, 117
  Classic Crab Cakes, 115
  Glazed and Suffused Mighty Macumbo
    Shrimp, 171
  Michael Jordan's 23 Peekytoe Crab
    Sandwich, 60–61
  Mom's Kebobs, 179
  Peter's Phyllo-Wrapped Gulf Prawns *à la*
    Lodge Club, 120–21
  The Queen's Wings, 94–95
Apple Cake, Miss Jan's Fantasy, 188–89
apple lore, 9
Apple Piagra, 208–9
Armstrong, Louis, 86
Art of Real Barbecuing, 175–76
Asparagus, Steamed Sesame, 130

Bacchus, 164
Baked Goods
  Apple Piagra, 208–9
  Bet on It Banana Bread, 12
  Blind Date Carrot Cake with Butter Cream
    Frosting, 190–91
  Bliss-Out Blackberry Cobbler, 194
  Bradley Ogden's Nectarine Blueberry
    Crisp, 194–95
  Casablanca Cheesecake, 200–201
  Champion Chip Cookies, 183
  French Stud Muffins, 10–11
  Gramma Orr's Buttermilk Biscuits, 14
  Lemon Heaven Meringue Pie, 204–5
  Miss Jan's Fantasy Apple Cake, 188–89
  Sensuous Cinnamon Rolls, 7–8
  Sweet Potato American Pie, 203
baking tips, 192
Banana Bread, Bet on It, 12
banana bread lore, 11–12
Baptized Bird with Harvest Butter Rum
  Stuffing, 111–12
Barbara's Jalapeño Jelly, 17–18

Barbecue and Grilled Fare
  Ahi-Ahi Quickie with Ruby Glaze, 172
  Art of Real Barbecuing, 175–76
  Big Easy Creole Seasoning, 87
  Bob Weir's Peanut Satay Sauce, 168
  Bravado Bud Butt Chicken, 163
  Chicken Waikiki Beach Supreme, 166
  Glazed and Suffused Mighty Macumbo
    Shrimp, 171
  Hamburger du Paradis à Mourir, 161
  Michael Jordan's 23 Delmonico, 178
  Mom's Kebobs, 179
  Pistachio-Crusted Grilled Satay Scallops,
    168
  Poker Club Asian Flank Steak, 174
  Uncle Sven's Secret Sauce, 164
barbecue festivals, 174
Barbecuing, The Art of Real, 175–76
Batali, Mario, 63, 69–72, 133, 214
beans, 86
  Coach Pate's Cajun R&R, 87–88
Beef
  Chili of Champions, 39–40
  Dan Healy's Weapons Grade Meatballs and
    Spaghetti, 74–75
  Guastavino's Cuban Tripe Stew, 139–40
  Hamburger du Paradis à Mourir, 161
  Healthy JO's, 52–53
  John Elway's Hamburger Soup, 37
  Lasagna Cubana, 75–76
  Magnificent Meatloaf, 142, 207

Michael Jordan's 23 Delmonico, 178
  Mom's Kebobs, 179
  Poker Club Asian Flank Steak, 174
  Slottsstek (Swedish Pot Roast), 146
  Unreal Red's Hot Dogs, 54–55
beef stew lore, 138
Belgian Waffles, Norwegian, 25
Ben's Fantasy Pecan-Covered Breasts, 106
Bet on It Banana Bread, 12
Big Cheese Grilled Grande, 58
Big Easy Creole Seasoning, 87
Biker Billy (Bill Hufnagle), 169, 212
Biscuits, Gramma Orr's Buttermilk, 14
Blind Date Carrot Cake with Butter Cream
  Frosting, 190–91
Bliss-Out Blackberry Cobbler, 194
Breads
  Bet on It Banana Bread, 12
  Johnny Cake Corn Bread, 16
  King Toast with Queen Peach Sauce, 22–23
  Sensuous Cinnamon Rolls, 7–8
Breakfast Fare
  Barbara's Jalapeño Jelly, 17–18
  Bet on It Banana Bread, 12
  Effortless Omelet, 30–31
  Falls Mill Uptown Cheese Grits, 27
  French Stud Muffins, 10–11
  Gramma Orr's Buttermilk Biscuits, 14
  Johnny Cake Corn Bread, 16
  King Toast with Queen Peach Sauce,
    22–23

Norwegian Belgian Waffles, 25
Quiche des Vrais Hommes, 33–34
Sensuous Cinnamon Rolls, 7–8
Silver Dollar Slapjacks with Wild Blue
  Sauce, 20–21
Bob Weir's Peanut Satay Sauce, 168
Bohemian B.L.T. Pizza, 85
Bonnie's restaurant, 145
Bradley Ogden's Nectarine Blueberry Crisp,
  194–95
Bravado Bud Butt Chicken, 163
Brillat-Savarin, 89, 110
Brown, Alton, 24
Bucatini all'Amatriciana, Mario Batali's, 70
Butter Cream Frosting, 191
Buttermilk Dream Sauce, 188

Cadillac Ranch Dip, 96
Caen, Herb, 38
Caesar Salad lore, 50
Caesar Salad, Portabello, 51
Cakes
  angel food, 185
  Blind Date Carrot Cake with Butter Cream
    Frosting, 190–91
  Casablanca Cheesecake, 200–201
  devil's food, 185, 187
  Miss Jan's Fantasy Apple Cake, 188–89
  Tiramisu, 197
Caldereta del Mar, 134–35
canning tips, 17–18

Carrot Cake with Butter Cream Frosting,
  Blind Date, 190–91
Carrots, Sweet Baby, 101–2
Casablanca Cheesecake, 200–201
Casanova Clam Linguine, 79–80
Casseroles
  Lasagna Cubana, 75–76
  Luxury Tuna Casserole, 67–68
  Maglooba, 108–9
  Magnificent Meatloaf, 142, 207
  Majestic Macaroni and Cheese, 65–66
  Shivani's Outrageous Potatoes, 143
Ceviche Ecuatoriano, 117
Champion Chip Cookies, 183
Cheeses
  Big Cheese Grilled Grande, 58
  Casablanca Cheesecake, 200–201
  Falls Mill Uptown Cheese Grits, 27
  Glazed and Suffused Mighty Macumbo
    Shrimp, 171
  Majestic Macaroni and Cheese, 65–66
  Mascarpone in a Pinch, 198
  Monte Cristo Disneyland Sandwich, 57
Cheesecake, Casablanca, 200–201
Chicken
  Ben's Fantasy Pecan-Covered Breasts, 106
  Bravado Bud Butt Chicken, 163
  Chicken Artichoke Enchiladas, 102–4
  Chicken Dumplings Divine, 98–99
  Chicken Waikiki Beach Supreme, 166
  L. J.'s Jewish Chinese Chicken, 101

Chicken *continued:*
  Maglooba, 108–9
  The Queen's Wings, 94–95
  Tom Lagana's Original Chicken Soul
    Soup, 45
Chicken Artichoke Enchiladas, 102–4
Chicken Dumplings Divine, 98–99
chicken fried steak, 28
Chicken Waikiki Beach Supreme, 166
Chili of Champions, 39–40
Churchill, Winston, 1–2
cioppino, 133
Chocolate
  Champion Chip Cookies, 183
  Hot Fudge Double Diablo Chocolate
    Brownie Eskimo Pie Sundae, 186
  Tiramisu, 197
chocolate lore, 184–85, 187
cinnamon lore, 6, 9
Cinnamon Rolls, Sensuous, 6–8
Claiborne, Craig, 38
Clam Chowder, Noble New England, 42–43
Classic Crab Cakes, 115
Clemens, Samuel (*see also* Mark Twain), 19,
  148
Coach Pate's Cajun R&R, 87–88
Cobblers and Crisps
  Bliss-Out Blackberry Cobbler, 194
  Bradley Ogden's Nectarine Blueberry
    Crisp, 194–95

Cookies
  Champion Chip Cookies, 183
  Margie's Cowboy Cookies, 182, 207
Coolidge, Calvin, 18
Corn Bread, Johnny Cake, 16
Costner, Kevin, 100
Cowboy Cookies, Margie's, 182, 207
Crab
  Classic Crab Cakes, 115
  Michael Jordan's 23 Peekytoe Crab
    Sandwich, 60–61
Cream of Wheat, 26
Cruise, Tom, 77–78, 193

**D**an Healy's Weapons Grade Meatballs and
  Spaghetti, 74–75
Delmonico, Michael Jordan's 23, 178
Desserts (*see also* Baked Goods; Cakes;
  Cobblers and Crisps; Pies)
  Apple Piagra, 208–9
  Bet on It Banana Bread, 12
  Blind Date Carrot Cake with Butter Cream
    Frosting, 190–91
  Bliss-Out Blackberry Cobbler, 194
  Bradley Ogden's Nectarine Blueberry
    Crisp, 194–95
  Casablanca Cheesecake, 200–201
  Champion Chip Cookies, 183
  Diablo Hot Fudge, 186
  Gramma Orr's Buttermilk Biscuits, 14

Lemon Heaven Meringue Pie, 204–5
Miss Jan's Fantasy Apple Cake, 188–89
Sweet Potato American Pie, 203
Tiramisu, 197
devil's food cake, 185, 187
Diablo Hot Fudge, 186
Dionysus, 164
Dip, Cadillac Ranch, 96

**E**ffortless Omelet, 30–31
Eisenhower, David and Julie Nixon, 11
Eisenhower, "Ike," 138
Eggs
Effortless Omelet, 30–31
Quiche des Vrais Hommes, 33–34
egg lore, 31, 53
eggplant (Maglooba), 108–9
Ellington, Duke, 29
Elton John, 64
Elvis (Presley), 53
Elway, John, 35–37, 219
Emeril Lagasse, 113
Enchiladas, Chicken Artichoke, 102–4
Escoffier, Auguste, 40

**F**alls Mill Uptown Cheese Grits, 27
Fish (*see also* Crab; Seafood)
Ahi-Ahi Quickie with Ruby Glaze, 172
Caldereta del Mar, 134–135
Joanne Woodward's Sole Cabernet, 123

Kathy's Fresh Catch, 126
Luxury Tuna Casserole, 67–68
Wild Alaska Honey-Lime Salmon, 132
Fong-Torres, Ben, 105–6
Ford, Gerald, 24
Franklin, Benjamin, 15
French Stud Muffins, 10–11
French toast lore, 22
Freud, Sigmund, 89
Frostings
Butter Cream Frosting, 191
Buttermilk Dream Sauce, 188
In the Clouds Meringue, 204–5

**G**arcia, Jerry, 55
Gere, Richard, 181
German Home-Fried New Potatoes, 151
Glazed and Suffused Mighty Macumbo
Shrimp, 171
Gore, Al and Tipper, 100
Gramma Orr's Buttermilk Biscuits, 14
Grateful Dead, 55, 73, 167
Great Crater Gravy, 155
grilled cheese sandwich lore, 56, 58
Grits, Falls Mill Uptown Cheese, 27
Guastavino's restaurant, 13–14, 138
Guastavino's Cuban Tripe Stew, 139–40

**H**alston, 185
Hamburger du Paradis à Mourir, 161

Hamburger Soup, John Elway's, 37
hangover cure, 116–17
Harvest Butter Rum Stuffing, 111–12
Healthy JO's, 52–53
Healy, Dan, 73
Hollandaise Sauce, Joanne's, 123–24
Honey-Rosemary Lamb Chops, 153
Hope, Bob, 100
Hot Dogs, Unreal Red's, 54–55
Hot Fudge, Diablo, 186
Hot Fudge Double Diablo Chocolate
  Brownie Eskimo Pie Sundae, 186

In the Clouds Meringue, 204–5

Jackson, Andrew, 18
Jalapeño Jelly, Barbara's, 17–18
Jefferson, Thomas, 18, 24, 156, 160
Jelly, Barbara's Jalapeño, 17–18
Joanne's Hollandaise Sauce, 123–24
Joanne Woodward's Sole Cabernet, 123
John Elway's Hamburger Soup, 37
Johnny Cake Corn Bread, 16
Johnson, Lyndon B., 160
Jordan, Michael, 60, 64, 177

Kathy's Fresh Catch, 126
Kennedy, Bobby, 185
Kennedy, John F., 41, 185

ketchup lore, 118, 141
King George VI, 54
King Toast with Queen Peach Sauce, 22–23

L. J.'s Jewish Chinese Chicken, 101
Lagana, Tom, 44–45
Lamb Chops, Honey-Rosemary, 153
Lark Creek Inn, 137, 193
Lasagna Cubana, 75–76
Lemon Heaven Meringue Pie, 204–5
Liberace, 138
Linguine (*see also* Pasta)
  Casanova Clam Linguine, 79–80
  Love Apple Linguine, 81–82, 207
  Tom Cruise's Linguine with Zesty Red
    Clam Sauce, 78–79
lobster, how to prepare for cooking,
  135
Love Apple Linguini, 81–82, 207
Lund, JoAnna M., 52–53, 213
Luxury Tuna Casserole, 67–68

Macaroni and cheese lore, 64
Macaroni and Cheese, Majestic, 65–66
Madge's Own Salad Dressing, 47
Maglooba, 108–9
Magnificent Meatloaf, the, 142, 207
Majestic Macaroni and Cheese, 65–66
Mandarin Scallops Stir Fry, 128

Margie's Cowboy Cookies, 182, 207
Mario Batali's Basic Tomato Sauce, 71
Mario Batali's Bucatini all'Amatriciana, 70
Mark Twain, 19, 148
Martin, Steve, 193
Mascarpone in a Pinch, 198
McConaughey, Matthew, 162
Meatballs and Spaghetti, Dan Healy's
  Weapons Grade, 74–75
Meatloaf, the Magnificent, 142, 207
Meringue, in the Clouds, 204–5
Michael Jordan's 23 (restaurant), 60–61,
  177–78
Michael Jordan's 23 Delmonico, 178
Michael Jordan's 23 Peekytoe Crab Sand-
  wich, 60–61
Miss Jan's Fantasy Apple Cake, 188–89
Mom's Kebobs, 179
Monte Cristo sandwich lore, 56–57
Monte Cristo Disneyland Sandwich, 57
Muffins, French Stud, 10–11
mushrooms (Risotto ai Funghi Porcini),
  90–91
mushroom lore, 89

Napoleon Bonaparte, 72, 109
Nectarine Blueberry Crisp, Bradley Ogden's,
  194–95
Newman, Paul, 44, 46, 86, 122
Nicholson, Jack, 145

Noble New England Clam Chowder, 42–43
Norwegian Belgian Waffles, 25
Notre Dame Fighting Irish football team, 144

Ogden, Bradley, 193–94, 212
Omelet, Effortless, 30–31
Orr, Daniel, 13–14, 138, 211, 213
Oscar of the Waldorf, 48
oyster lore, 114, 116

Paella, 107
pancakes (Silver Dollar Slapjacks), 20–21
pancake lore, 18–19
Pasta
  Casanova Clam Linguine, 79–80
  Dan Healy's Weapons Grade Meatballs and
    Spaghetti, 74–75
  Lasagna Cubana, 75–76
  Love Apple Linguini, 81–82, 207
  Majestic Macaroni and Cheese, 65–66
  Mario Batali's Basic Tomato Sauce, 71
  Mario Batali's Bucatini all'Amatriciana, 70
  Sparkling Scampi in Mascarpone Cream
    Sauce, 129
  Tom Cruise's Linguine with Zesty Red
    Clam Sauce, 78–79
Peanut Satay Sauce, Bob Weir's, 168
Pecan-Covered Breasts, Ben's Fantasy, 106
pepper lore, 169
Perfect Pie Dough, Double Crust, 208

Perkins, Peter Quah, 119–20
Peter's Phyllo-Wrapped Gulf Prawns *à la*
  Lodge Club, 120–21
Philly Cheesesteak, 59
Piagra, Apple, 208–9
Pies
  Apple Piagra, 208–9
  Double Crust Perfect Pie Dough, 208
  Lemon Heaven Meringue Pie, 204–5
  Sweet Potato American Pie, 203
pie shell, pre-baking, 206
Pistachio-Crusted Grilled Satay Scallops,
  168
Pizza
  Bohemian B.L.T. Pizza, 85
  Pizza Alla Zingara, 84
Pizza Alla Zingara, 84
Poker Club Asian Flank Steak, 174
Pork
  Bohemian B.L.T. Pizza, 85
  Guastavino's Cuban Tripe Stew, 139–40
  Mario Batali's Bucatini all'Amatriciana, 70
  Monte Cristo Disneyland Sandwich, 57
  Pork Chops in Stout, 149–50
  Unreal Red's Hot Dogs, 54–55
Pork Chops in Stout, 149–50
Portabello Caesar Salad, 51
Potatoes
  German Home-Fried New Potatoes, 151
  Regal Roasted Russet, The, 147

Shivani's Outrageous Potatoes, 143
  Spiced Garlic Spuds, 154
  Sweet Potato American Pie, 203
pot roast, Swedish (Slottsstek), 146
Poultry, (*see also* Chicken; Turkey)
  Baptized Bird with Harvest Butter Rum
    Stuffing, 111–12
  Ben's Fantasy Pecan-Covered Breasts, 106
  Bravado Bud Butt Chicken, 163
  Chicken Artichoke Enchiladas, 102–4
  Chicken Waikiki Beach Supreme, 166
  L. J.'s Jewish Chinese Chicken, 101
  The Queen's Wings, 94–95
Prawns *à la* Lodge Club, Peter's Phyllo-
  Wrapped Gulf, 120–21

Queen's Wings, 94–95
Quiche des Vrais Hommes, 33–34

Reagan, Ronald, 11, 64, 138, 141
red beans and rice lore, 86
Regal Roasted Russet, 147
Reynolds, Burt, 138
Rice and Risotto
  Coach Pate's Cajun R&R, 87–88
  Maglooba, 108–9
  Risotto ai Funghi Porcini, 90–91
  Sparkling Scampi in Mascarpone Cream
    Sauce, 129
Risotto ai Funghi Porcini, 90–91

Roosevelt, Eleanor, 54
Roosevelt, Franklin D., 18, 54
Rosengarten, David, 97, 214

Salads and Salad Dressings
  Cadillac Ranch Dip, 96
  Caesar Salad dressing, 51
  Madge's Own Salad Dressing, 47
  Portabello Caesar Salad, 51
  With-It Waldorf Salad, 49
Salmon
  Quiche des Vrais Hommes, 33–34
  Wild Alaska Honey-Lime Salmon, 132
Sandwiches
  Big Cheese Grilled Grande, 58
  Hamburger du Paradis à Mourir, 161
  Healthy JO's, 52–53
  Michael Jordan's 23 Peekytoe Crab
    Sandwich, 60–61
  Monte Cristo Disneyland Sandwich, 57
  Unreal Red's Hot Dogs, 54–55
sandwich lore, 52–56, 59
Sauces
  Almond Sauce, 158
  Bob Weir's Peanut Satay Sauce, 168
  Buttermilk Dream Sauce, 188
  Clam Sauce, Tom Cruise's Linguine with
    Zesty Red, 78–79
  Diablo Hot Fudge, 186
  Great Crater Gravy, 155

  Joanne's Hollandaise Sauce, 123–24
  Mario Batali's Basic Tomato Sauce, 71
  Mascarpone Cream Sauce, 129
  Queen Peach Sauce, 22–23
  Ruby Glaze, 172
  Sauce Supreme, 166
  Uncle Sven's Secret Sauce, 164
  Wild Blue Sauce, 20–21
Scallops, Pistachio-Crusted Grilled Satay,
  168
Scampi in Mascarpone Cream Sauce,
  Sparkling, 129
Seafood
  Caldereta del Mar, 134–35
  Casanova Clam Linguine, 79–80
  Ceviche Ecuatoriano, 117
  Classic Crab Cakes, 115
  Glazed and Suffused Mighty Macumbo
    Shrimp, 171
  Joanne Woodward's Sole Cabernet, 123
  Mandarin Scallops Stir Fry, 128
  Michael Jordan's 23 Peekytoe Crab Sand-
    wich, 60–61
  Noble New England Clam Chowder,
    42–43
  Peter's Phyllo-Wrapped Gulf Prawns *à la*
    Lodge Club, 120–21
  Pistachio-Crusted Grilled Satay Scallops,
    168
  Quiche des Vrais Hommes, 33–34

Seafood *continued:*
  Sparkling Scampi in Mascarpone Cream
    Sauce, 129
  Tom Cruise's Linguine with Zesty Red
    Clam Sauce, 78–79
  Wild Alaska Honey-Lime Salmon, 132
Seasoning, Big Easy Creole, 87
Sensuous Cinnamon Rolls, 7–8
Shivani's Outrageous Potatoes, 143
Silver Dollar Slapjacks with Wild Blue Sauce,
  20–21
Slottsstek (Swedish Pot Roast), 146
Smith, Andrew F., 33, 118, 175
Soups and Stews
  Caldereta del Mar, 134–35
  Chicken Dumplings Divine, 98–99
  Chili of Champions, 39–40
  Coach Pate's Cajun R&R, 87–88
  Guastavino's Cuban Tripe Stew, 139–40
  John Elway's Hamburger Soup, 37
  Noble New England Clam Chowder,
    42–43
  Tom Lagana's Original Chicken Soul
    Soup, 45
soup and stew lore, 40–41, 44, 97, 130,
  133, 138
Spaghetti, Dan Healy's Weapons Grade
  Meatballs and, 74–75
Spanish fly (*see also* aphrodisiacs), 114

Spanish Veal with Almond Sauce, 158
Sparkling Scampi in Mascarpone Cream
  Sauce, 129
Spiced Garlic Spuds, 154
Steak, Poker Club Asian Flank, 174
Steamed Sesame Asparagus, 130
Stir Fry, Mandarin Scallops, 128
Stuffing, Harvest Butter Rum, 111–12
Sweet Baby Carrots, 101–2
Sweet Potato American Pie, 203

Television Food Network, 24, 69, 97
Tiramisu, 197
Toast with Queen Peach Sauce, King, 22–23
Tomatoes
  Chili of Champions, 39–40
  Love Apple Linguini, 81–82, 207
  Mario Batali's Basic Tomato Sauce, 71
  Tom Cruise's Linguine with Zesty Red
    Clam Sauce, 78–79
tomato lore, 81
Tom Cruise's Linguine with Zesty Red Clam
  Sauce, 78–79
Tom Lagana's Original Chicken Soul Soup,
  45
Tripe Stew, Guastavino's Cuban, 139–40
trout (Kathy's Fresh Catch), 126
Truman, Harry, 2, 48, 64, 67, 141
Tuna Casserole, Luxury, 67–68

tuna noodle casserole lore, 2, 64, 67–68
Turkey
  Baptized Bird with Harvest Butter Rum
    Stuffing, 111–12
  Monte Cristo Disneyland Sandwich, 57

Uncle Sven's Secret Sauce, 164
Unreal Red's Hot Dogs, 54–55

Veal with Almond Sauce, Spanish, 158
Vegetables
  German Home-Fried New Potatoes, 151
  Regal Roasted Russet, the, 147
  Shivani's Outrageous Potatoes, 143
  Spiced Garlic Spuds, 154

Steamed Sesame Asparagus, 130
Sweet Baby Carrots, 101–2
Velveeta, 66

Waffle lore, 24
Waffles, Norwegian Belgian, 25
Waldorf Salad, With-It, 49
Weir, Bob, 167–68
Weir's Sauces, 212
Welcher, Dorismarie, 62, 94
Wheaties, 6
Wild Alaska Honey-Lime Salmon, 132
With-It Waldorf Salad, 49
Woodward, Joanne, 122–23

# Permissions

I am grateful for permission to excerpt from the following works and for the delicious enthusiasm everyone shared:

*Goddess in the Kitchen* by Margie Lapanja. Copyright © 1998 by Margaret Beiser Lapanja. Reprinted with permission of Conari Press.

*Eat Dangerously Cookbook* by Benjamin Lewis and Rodrigo Velloso. Copyright © 1999 by Hollander and Hechsher. Reprinted with permission of Hollander and Hechsher.

*Newman's Own Cookbook* by Paul Newman and A. E. Hotchner. Copyright © 1998 by Hole in the Wall Gang Fund, Inc. Reprinted with permission of Simon & Schuster.

*Wild Women in the Kitchen: 101 Rambunctious Recipes and 99 Tasty Tales* by The Wild Women Association. Copyright © 1996 by The Wild Women Association. Reprinted with permission of Conari Press.

"The Art of Real Barbecuing" reprinted with permission of Andrew F. Smith. "Big Cheese Grilled Grande" inspired by a recipe submitted by Ted Michon. "Bob Weir's Peanut Satay Sauce" reprinted with permission of Weir's Sauces. "Barbara's Jalapeño Jelly" reprinted with permission of Barbara Moniot. "Ben's Fantasy Pecan-Covered Breasts" and text reprinted with permission of Ben Fong-Torres. "Bohemian B.L.T. Pizza" inspired by a recipe submitted by Benet Terry. "Bradley Ogden's Nectarine Blueberry Crisp" reprinted with permission of Bradley Ogden. "Cadillac Ranch Dip" reprinted with permission of Nancy O'Connell. "Casanova Clam Linguine" reprinted with permission of DeAnn Grasinger. "Ceviche Ecuatoriano" inspired by a recipe submitted by Michael

J. Beiser and Patricio Aguirre. "Classic Crab Cakes" reprinted with permission of Bill Hull. "Coach Pate's Cajun R&R" inspired by a recipe submitted by Wayne Pate. "Dan Healy's Weapons Grade Meatballs and Spaghetti" reprinted with permission of Patti Healy. "Falls Mill Uptown Cheese Grits" reprinted with permission of John and Jane Lovett. "Gramma Orr's Buttermilk Biscuits" and "Guastavino's Cuban Tripe Stew" reprinted with permission of Daniel Orr. "Healthy JO's" reprinted with permission of JoAnna M. Lund. "John Elway's Hamburger Soup" reprinted with permission of John Elway. "Lasagna Cubana" inspired by a recipe submitted by David Mogelefsy. "Lemon Heaven Meringue Pie" courtesy of Grace Fuller. "L. J.'s Jewish Chinese Chicken" courtesy of L. Jay. "Luxury Tuna Casserole" courtesy of Michael J. Beiser. "Madge's Own Salad Dressing" reprinted with permission of Mark Englund. "Maglooba" inspired by a recipe submitted by Jeff Ogren. "Mario Batali's Bucatini all'Amatriciana" and "Mario Batali's Basic Tomato Sauce" reprinted with permission of Mario Batali. "Michael Jordan's 23 Delmonico" and "Michael Jordan's 23 Peekytoe Crab Sandwich" reprinted with permission of Michael Jordan's 23. "Miss Jan's Fantasy Apple Cake" reprinted with permission of Jan Sargent. "Mom's Kebobs" inspired by a recipe submitted by Murray Williams' mother. "Peter's Phyllo-Wrapped Gulf Prawns à la Lodge Club" reprinted with permission of Peter Perkins. "Poker Club Asian Flank Steak" reprinted with permission of Don McIlraith. "Pork Chops in Stout" courtesy of Susan Strachan. "Sparkling Scampi in Mascarpone Cream Sauce" inspired by a recipe submitted by Nancy O'Connell. "Shivani's Outrageous Potatoes" courtesy of Shivani Grail Atkinson. "Sweet Baby Carrots" courtesy of Anthea Stiegler. "Spanish Veal with Almond Sauce" courtesy of John Schneider. "Tom Lagana's Original Chicken Soul Soup" reprinted with permission of Tom Lagana. "Tiramisu" reprinted with permission of GraceAnn Walden. "Uncle Sven's Secret Sauce" courtesy of Kristina Hill. "Unreal Red's Hot Dogs" invented and submitted by Charlie Girsch. "Wild Alaska Honey-Lime Salmon" inspired by a recipe submitted by Jim Plumbridge.

# Served with Love

A portion of proceeds from sales of *Food Men Love* will be donated to the following organizations:

**The Elway Foundation**
12835 East Arapahoe Road
Tower II, Suite 700
Englewood, CO 80112
Phone: 303 790-7300
*The John and Janet Elway Foundation is dedicated to the prevention and treatment of child abuse and secures funding to benefit the Kempe Children's Foundation and F.A.C.E.S.*

**The Further Foundation**
c/o Barbara Whitestone
P. O. Box 1688
Glen Ellen, CA 95442
*The Furthur Foundation supports the environment, children's education, and homeless causes.*

**Mothers' Voices**
165 West 46th Street, Suite 701
New York, NY 10036
Phone: 888 MVOICES or 212 730-2777
Web: *www.mvoices.org*
*Mothers' Voices is a national, grassroots organization dedicated to mobilizing parents as educators and advocates in the fight against AIDS. To order a copy of their fundraising cookbook,* Comfort Foods from Mothers' Voices, *please contact them directly*